COMMUNITY COLLEGE
CURRICULUM AND TEACHING

By

Dr. Marlow Ediger
Professor Emeritus
Division of Education
Truman State University
P.O. Box 417, 201 W, 22nd St
North Newton KS 67117
United States of America

Dr. Digumarti Bhaskara Rao
M.Sc., M.A., M.A., M.Ed., Ph.D.
Reader
R.V.R. College of Education
Srinivasa Nagar Colony
Guntur–522 006
&
Member
Board of Studies in Education
Acharya Nagarjuna University
Nagarjuna Nagar
Andhra Pradesh
(India)

D P H

DISCOVERY PUBLISHING HOUSE
NEW DELHI-110002

First Published – 2006
Reprinted – 2015

ISBN: 978-81-8356-053-5

Community College
Curriculum and Teaching

Published by:
DISCOVERY PUBLISHING HOUSE PVT. LTD.
4383/4B, Ansari Road, Darya Ganj
New Delhi-110 002 (India)
Phone: +91-11-23279245, 43596064-65
Fax: +91-11-23253475
E-mail: discoverypublishinghouse@gmail.com
sales@discoverypublishinggroup.com
web: www.discoverypublishinggroup.com

Printed at:
Infinity Imaging Systems
Delhi

Preface

Education has become a part and parcel of human enterprise. Several stages of education have spread over every nook and corner of the society. Now-a-days, the colleges are playing a crucial role in educating rural community. These rural community colleges that provide higher education in country-side communities need special care and attention. Some of the issues concerned to community colleges are discussed in this book to bring awareness among the community college personnel and public.

Marlow Ediger
Bhaskara Rao

Contents

1

Administration and the Community College Curriculum

Advocates of responsible change in course offerings in higher education believes strongly in improving the curriculum. There is considerable emphasis placed upon faculty being teachers/ instructors rather than researchers. Dedicated faculty who are in the instructional arena then need to be in the offing. These instructors must place high value on university students achieving at a high level since regular faculty members rather than graduate assistants teach students. More stress then should be placed upon hiring faculty who have as a major goal the teaching of students rather than being in the area of research. However, there appear to be several slogans here in viewing faculty members in a university.

One slogan pertains to those who are teaching faculty as well as regular members of the faculty and are capable instructors. It almost singles out the researcher who also teaches but does not do a satisfactory job of instruction. Perhaps, research and teaching are not at loggerheads with each other. Thus the research that is done should be in one's area of expertise and the results may be used in the academic areas taught. Additionally, there is much motivation here if the research results are published. Manuscripts and textbooks published might well provide the encouragement to maintain and stay in the higher education teaching profession. Feelings of being a recognised professional can assist the professor/writer to distinguish the self and develop an excellent self concept. Quality in teaching university students might well be an end result. Much reinforcement is in evidence if an instructor receives notice that a manuscript has been accepted for publication.

The professor who does no research may do very little to prepare for each day and unit of teaching. There is a misunderstanding in that instructors who teach well do no research. This can be very erroneous. However, hopefully, these instructors who do no research will truly prepare well for teaching and be dedicated instructor. It certainly can also be that researcher has little interest in teaching students. To appraise instructors, one has to evaluate professors on an individual basis. Very little is done to evaluate professor competency in the classroom on the higher education level.

Student Ratings of Professors

Perhaps, the most common approach in assessing instructor competence in teaching is to use university student ratings of each class taught. Standards used to rate instructors may be either standardised or developed by the university. Generally, the students rate the instructor at the end of the semester for each course taught. Better it would be to rate the instructor more so toward the beginning of the course so that feedback can be given to the instructor who teaches the course. If ratings are given by students toward the last day of the course, the results are not valid for the next set of students taught since they are different learners as compared to the ones who did the rating.

Seemingly, students are not accountable for ratings given. Each student is anonymous and can not be asked to justify ratings given. Thus if a low rating is given to "This class is as difficult as others I have taken," the student does not need to indicate what the instructor can do to improve instruction. Or if students are asked to rate an instructor on "starting and stopping classes on time," the following are points of debate:

1. Did the instructor follow one, and if so which one, or did he/she follow both standards such as "starting *or* stopping classes on time?"
2. What happened between the two points of beginning and ending a class on time? The time here is crucial in terms of instructional time.
3. Do students truly try to answer each item conscientiously? This question applies to any item on the form to appraise the quality of instruction.
4. Are students knowledgeable about evaluating an instructor in higher cognitive processes such as critical and creative thinking, as well as problem solving. A conference involving the university student and the instructor might clarify how an instructor would teach if these higher levels of thinking would be stressed in teaching-learning situations.
5. Why must student evaluations by anonymous in terms of who responded how? There are implications that instructors are highly vindictive. We believe many instructors truly want to know how well students perceive the former's teaching quality. The evaluations become hazy unless there are conferences to clarify items for appraisal as well as why responses were made as they were by students.

We are not opposed to students evaluating instruction quality. It is a must in the university evaluation process. Democratic tenets stress that individuals be involved in decision making pertaining to what affects them personally. Instruments used need to be carefully developed if constructed on the university level. Vague, ridiculous items should definitely not be on the evaluation form. If the evaluative instrument has been standardized, the items therein need to be carefully reviewed prior to it being to purchased. Certainly, the items used to appraise instructional performances should be relevant and diagnostic. Instructors should be obtain feedback on how to do a better a job of teaching. However when the evaluative results come back to the instructor, he/she must do the best possible to make sense of the feedback as well as improve teaching-learning situations.

Improving Procedures of Instruction and Evaluation

Generally very little is done on the university level to improve the quality of instruction. An assumption has been that instructors with earned doctorates are carefully hired and need no further inservice education. The assumption is erroneous in that the employed individual for a university position will put the best foot forward to secure an appointment in an interview setting. To be sure, there are many instructors who have done well in instruction based on designated university personnel observing the candidate's credentials and interviewing posture. Many universities are now having candidates for employment teach a class or conduct a workshop prior to being employed. Interested faculty may than observe the quality of teaching being displayed and provide information to those involved in the hiring process as to how well the prospective candidate did in teaching or conducting a workshop. There is a greater chance that an employed instructor will do much better in the instructional arena if he/she had to demonstrate proficiency prior to being hired.

After being employed, the instructor needs to develop a plan for continuous inservice development. A committee needs to be in charge of approving the inservice growth plan. We recommend the following as possibilities for an instructor to have a plan for continuous inservice education:

1. attend two professional conventions per year pertaining to one's academic area of specialty. Information should be available to the degree that knowledge acquired at the convention is being used in classroom teaching or assisting students in course work;
2. do research in one's subject matter specialty and incorporate new ideas into the curriculum. Research done should not hinder the quality of classroom

teaching. Rather classroom performance is improved due to research results obtained. The instructor should attempt to publish research results in a refereed journal. It is a true motivator to have a journal article or textbook published;

3. work with a colleague to improve the quality of classroom teaching through observations made and quality standards used to appraise performance and improve instruction;
4. have a planned series of meetings with colleagues in the same area of academic specialty to establish goals and means of attaining the goals to improve instruction;
5. update syllabi for each class taught. The syllabi should show clearly stated objectives, learning opportunities, appraisal procedures, and relevant bibliography entries for each unit taught. The purpose of the syllabi is to enhance optimal learner progress. The syllabi contains questions for students to answer prior to each day's lessons and discussions.

Newly appointed faculty need to experience continuous progress in achievement after appointment.

The Dean of Instruction and Instructional Improvement

When I (Ediger) began teaching on the university level, by beliefs were that the dean of instruction should be a leader on improving instruction for higher education students. Instead, a dean of instruction is much more concerned about the paperwork involved in getting the university ready for a visit by an accreditation group. Thus instructors are to file with the dean's office all updated syllabi written for courses taught. Tests given are also to be filed. Included in the self study are the numerous parts of the writeup that the accreditation organisation requires. The dean also meets once a month with the different division heads of university. Discussions here centre on necessary work that needs to be completed by each division. There are also different committee that a dean heads such as the undergraduate council, the graduate council, and the faculty senate. These councils/senate consider new and modified course offerings that a division wishes to have approved. Nowhere, however, is there talk and discussion on direct ways of improving the quality of instruction. My thinking is that the office of the dean should be in charge of improving teaching and learning in the course offerings of the university. It is one things to emphasise the written curriculum for accreditation organisations, the heads of different divisions in the university, as well as the diverse councils/faculty senate, but quite a different item to stress faculty growth in teaching university students.

We recommend that the office of the dean be responsible for stressing quality in each course offered on the campus as well as in extension work. The following approaches may be used to improve instruction:

1. a qualified person observing and evaluating the quality of instruction in a classroom. Results of the evaluation based on definite recommended criteria should be shared with the instructor. Future observational visits could reveal if there is improvement in teaching;
2. video-taping teaching performance and critiquing the results by a competent person. Feedback to the instructor is a must so that improvement is a definite possibility in teaching;
3. mini-lessons taught and appraised by peers. The purpose here again is to provide results to the instructor so that improvement in teaching is a definite possibility;
4. inservice meetings held pertaining to the improvement of instruction. Perhaps, an unenthused instructor has never considered methods of teaching other than lecture. Here at these inservice meetings, there are opportunities to use other approaches in teaching university students;

5. self-evaluation by the instructor. The instructor needs to be knowledgeable about quality to use in teaching and in the evaluation process. Video-taping and/or cassette recording may be used by the instructor for self evaluation. Continuous appraisal here is necessary so that growth and achievement are in evidence.

For each of the above means to improve instruction, the dean needs to take a leadership role to encourage improvement of instruction. Promotion to higher ranks should take into heavy consideration achievement in teaching as well as publication records. Teaching and research/publication should definitely compliment each other since the results of the latter can and should be used in improving teaching quality.

Criteria to Use in the Evaluating Processes

The dean of instruction must take a leadership role in assisting instructors to understand the teaching-learning process. Workshops conducted to improve the quality of teaching are musts on any university campus. We recommend the following criteria for instructors to emphasise to improve instruction:

1. Instructors need to secure the attention of students in the classroom setting. If learners do not attend, they cannot achieve well. Instructors need to engage students so that active involvement in learning is in evidence. Learning opportunities involving discussions can assist students to become active participants in learning. We recommend that instructors become highly skilled in having students engage in critical thinking. When thinking critically, students apply and use knowledge acquired so that it is not forgotten. With critical thinking, students appraise the accuracy of subject matter discussed. They compare and contrast what is being discussed with additional reputable reference sources. Bias of content discussed is detected in critical thinking.

Facts is separated from fiction, as well as each idea discussed is appraised in terms of worth to solve problems.

We also recommend that instructors become thoroughly familiar with creative thinking methods of instruction. With creative teaching, new methods of instruction are emphasised. A variety of procedures are then being stressed in teaching students. Lecture methods should not predominate. Discussions should be emphasised where by the instructor encourages inductive methods of teaching with induction, students discover knowledge through diverse approaches. One approach can be brainstorming whereby university students come up with numerous ideas pertaining to the meaning of subject matter, concepts, and generalisations. Brainstorming emphasises responses pertaining to the meaning of selected content be generated by learners. No value judgement is made pertaining to each response. No duplications nor repetitions of responses should be in evidence. It becomes increasingly more complex to come up with diversity of meaning as the brainstorming activity progresses. Ultimately each responses can be appraised in terms of accuracy. Perhaps, additional reference sources will need to be used to appraise selected brainstormed ideas. Spontaneity in response is wanted here so that university students are actively engaged in learning, not passive recipients of knowledge.

With creative thinking, novel answers are needed. Old, "tried and true" answers may not work in a new situation. Students need to be flexible in finding answers to questions. Originality, novelty, uniqueness, and newness are key concepts for instructors to emphasise in creative thinking.

2. Purpose for learning needs to stressed by the instructor. With purpose, learners feel that reasons

to learn exist. Content is not acquired then due only to the requirements of the instructor, but there are needs to be met in obtaining subject matter, concepts, generalisations, and main ideas. There are several ways that the instructor may emphasise purpose for learning. One way is for the instructor to state deductively why it is important for students to acquire selected content. This need not take up much time. Rather, quickly and concisely, the instructor can state why learners need to achieve certain relevant ideas. A second approach in having university students perceive purpose in learning is for the instructor to raise a few questions as to why the former should feel that selected content is valuable to learn. This takes a little longer in time for students to perceive purpose as compared to deduction procedures. The instructor will want to vary approaches in guiding students to perceive purpose in learning.

A third procedure in having university students perceive purpose in learning is for the instructor to use extrinsic rewards. Praise used by the instructor for quality responses of university students tends to be a motivator. Securing good test results encourages learners to do well. The test or evaluation procedures needs to be announced a few days prior to its being given so that motivation is there for the student to study, achieve, and learn. Extra work done by a student pertaining to a demanding project, can receive additional credit in the appraisal process. The completed project or activity must be evaluated in terms of quality criteria. Grades received stress reinforcement theory in teaching-learning situations. Extrinsic rewards are then in evidence.

We believe students learn best when intrinsic motivation, rather than extrinsic motivation, is present. With intrinsic motivation, students have an inward desire to learn and attain. Learning is its very own reward, rather than some external factor. If I study hard because the inward need to do so is there, no doubt the best achievement possible will then be in evidence. However, the instructor must motivate all students in class to do their best possible on an individual basis. Not all students are motivated intrinsically.

3. Interest is a powerful factor in learning. With interest, effort can come forth from each student. What if student interest is weak and lagging? Here the instructor needs to think of ways to stimulate interest in learning. To do this, the instructor may stress a problem solving strategy of instruction. Ideally, the student should identify a problem directly related to the topic being discussed in class. The problem should be adequately delimited so that problem solving can be stressed. After problem selection, data or information in answer to the problem should be gathered. A variety or reference sources need to be used here. Journal articles, textbook content, and audio-visual aids might be used to acquired necessary content. A hypothesis should then result to answer the problem area. The hypothesis needs testing through the use of additional reference sources. If necessary, revisions to the hypothesis may be made. Problem solving emphasises a higher cognitive level objective for student attainment. Generally, students are highly engaged in learning when problem solving is stressed. Interest and enthusiasm are and can be very high in these kinds of activities.

Inservice Education in Higher Education

Generally, inservice education for faculty is minimised on the university level. But, this should not be the case. Each instructor should experience workshops devoted to doing a better job of teaching. Members in the workshop should choose which problems should be identified and solved in teaching-learning situations. The general session should stress the identification of these problem areas. Instructors need to be active participants in the general session. For any group or committee to function well, definite criteria should be emphasised to secure input from all. Thus the following standards are vital to stress in a large group/committee endeavour:

1. stay on the topic being discussed. If digressions occur, much wasting of time can be an end result. Time should be used wisely so that instructors can zero in on relevant problems to solve. This does not mean that instructors hurry through any discussion being emphasised. It does take time to think any analyse what has been said. However, to divert from what is being discussed in terms of topic being pursued does take unnecessary time. Perhaps, those who digress from the topic being pursued can visit with each other at a later time.

2. use interaction rather than coaction. With interaction, ideas flow freely within the participants, not between two or three members serving in the group or committee. The chairperson's role should be to see that what is being discussed moves among all participants and actively involves each member. If no chairperson has been designated, ideas may come from what is known as situational leadership. That is to say that whoever is actively participating is the leader at that time, followed by sequential instructors who clarify, add to, or evaluate that which was stated previously. Thus leadership emerges among participants depending on who is contributing to the discussion. It is still the responsibility of participants to secure the active involvement of each instructor.

3. accept each person and each contribution made with respect. There is no role for one who treats others with disrespect when democracy is being stressed in

a group/committee endeavour. Being courteous and considerate are musts in any cooperative endeavour. If negative comments are made by anyone, participation will tend to go downhill and democratic tenets are no longer in evidence. Thus the processes of good cooperation are necessary so that conclusions reached truly represent the work of all who are considering a problem area.

4. accurate notes of each meeting should be recorded by a secretary. The recorded notes should be read back to the group/committee members to ensure that accuracy is there in summarising what has been discussed. Summaries should be photocopied and made available to each instructor as well as to other groups at work.

After the general session has been completed, faculty members may volunteer to work on the committee of their choice involving problems selected in the general session. There are definite preferences and needs that each participant has in choosing which problem area to work on. Reference sources, adequate in number, must be available for each committee to function well. Consultant assistance is recommended. Certainly, needed data and human guidance is necessary in order for a committee to locate and decide upon answers to identified problem areas, identified in the general session. Committees need to report to each other through reports provided by the recorder or another designated person. Quality communication is a must when diverse committees are at work. Committees can learn much from each other.

In addition to the general session and committee endeavours, individual instructor task selection is a must. Instructors differ from each other in terms of needs in the instructional arena. Thus an instructor should choose a problem area that is personally relevant. He/she then should acquire information from the workshop library which assists in securing necessary information. The ultimate goal in workshop endeavours is to improve the quality of teaching university students. Opportunities should be there to share content with others when an instructor works on a problem area of his/her own choosing.

In Closing

The dean of instruction has a vital role to play in improving the quality of teaching and learning. He/she needs to possess qualities and knowledge pertaining to raising university student achievement. The dean must be very understanding of ingredients that make for excellence in instruction. All instruction is guided by theories of instruction. Thus, something assists each person in making curricular decisions and that something is theory.

Rating of the instructor's teaching by students need to be improved upon so that the former receives clear communication of the quality of instruction provided as well as what to improve upon in the instructional arena.

The dean of instruction should provide a leadership role in guiding a plan of inservice education for faculty, starting with the time of employment, a variety of means of improve the self in teaching should be in the offing in the inservice plan.

The instructor has vital facets of instruction to follow when securing the attention, purposes, and interests of university students in the classroom setting. Workshops can be an excellent way of guiding instructional improvement on the part of instructors. A general session, committee endeavours, and individual choice of tasks can provide a well rounded possibility for inservice education. Committee members need to follow recommended criteria when discussing and solving problem areas pertaining to instruction. Each university student should attain as much as possible in the curriculum.

2

Faculty Development in the Community College

Faculty development must be ongoing in the community college. There are continual changes in the societal arena and the curriculum needs to incorporate positive changes. Otherwise, the community college curriculum might well become outdated. Selected educators state that the community college, along with other institutions of education and learning, should take the lead in improving the societal arena and not reflect the positive in society only. Thus the community college may be proactive or reactive in curriculum development. Whichever philosophical point of view that is taken, the community college faculty and administration must be updated through quality approaches in inservice education.

Faculty Inservice Education in the Community College

Instructors need to engage in self appraisal continuously. There are numerous facets of self appraisal. The instructor may desire to evaluate course objectives presently being emphasised. These objectives must emphasise relevant knowledge, skills, and attitudes. Trivia and outdated objectives need to be eliminated. Careful analysis of each objective stressed in teaching and learning must pass scrutiny in terms of being salient and utilitarian. Skills objectives should emphasise using the knowledge that has been acquired. Application goals are then being stressed in ongoing lessons and units of instruction.

Skills of critical and creative thinking as well as problem solving are always useful in school and in society. Whatever is done requires critical thought in that individuals make comparisons and contrasts as well as separate the accurate from the inaccurate, facts from opinions, and reality from that which is fictional. Reflecting upon what was done or read also requires critical thinking.

Creative thinking emphasises originality, the new, and the novel. Progress in education and in society many times comes from those who come up with modified or new ways of knowing, doing, and feeling. Community college instructors should provide ample opportunities for students to achieve in the area of creative thought.

Problem solving may incorporate critical and creative thinking. To engage in problem solving, instructors need to guide students to identify significant problem areas. These problems are identified in context, that is within the framework of the ongoing lesson presentation. Data or information is acquired to solve the problem area, a hypothesis results in answer to the problem, and the hypothesis is tested and revised as necessary.

The attitudinal dimension of objectives for student attainment results from success, satisfaction, achievement, and sequential progress of the learners in the community college curriculum.

Arthur H. Cohen (1993) emphasises the importance of a general education programme which stresses the nonconventional courses of a general community college curriculum. He believes that a present day general education curriculum should place much importance on gender equity, ethnic studies, and global education which previous curricula had slighted. The Great Books could be a part of the general education community college offerings. Increased integration of subject matter should be inherent in curriculum revision. A problem, however, exists in that there are so many separate units and departments offering general education. Thus complexity is in evidence when the different departments and units plan together in attempting to relate subject matter taught in community college course work.

Faculty inservice education might well be emphasised in a planned series of meetings whereby instructors in involved course work would attempt to integrated subject matter from relevant courses. Faculty members in committee settings should view their own syllabi and study guides for students, to determine if updating and revisions need to be made of content taught. Adequate reference sources must be available to guide faculty in decision making. Leadership is necessary to stimulate and guide faculty to modify and revise as need in the objectives, learning opportunities, and appraisal procedures stressed in each course.

Don Cohen (1993) writes about "Standards for Curriculum and Pedagogical Reform in Two Year College and Lower Division Mathematics," developed by their Task Force. The Task Force in making recommendations focused on core content for community college students to achieve in mathematics. The core would consist of number, symbol, geometric, function, probability and statistics, and problem solving sense. Standards for students and faculty in mathematics are discussed.

Faculty need to identify vital content for student attainment as well as goals for faculty to achieve in teaching-learning situations. Core content of any discipline provides the framework for understanding an academic discipline. (Bruner, 1968) was an early advocate of mathematics, among others, identifying structural ideas that all students should achieve. These key ideas or core content would serve as a guide for developing statements of objectives for learners to attain. These structural ideas would be emphasised at increasingly levels of complexity as students progress to higher levels of attainment. Thus there would be agreement by mathematicians in terms of what is vital for students to achieve in mathematics. Bruner emphasised an inductive procedure of learning due to professional mathematicians also attaining subject matter inductively. The National Council Teachers of Mathematics (1989) identified a set of standards or objectives for pupils to achieve in the school setting in their publication *Curriculum and Evaluation Standards for School Mathematics*. Here is another example of mathematicians being involved in determining what is vital for learners to achieve in the curriculum. These objectives might well be perceived as representing a core of facts, concepts, and generalisations for learners to attain within the framework of critical and creative thinking as well as problem solving.

Cooperative endeavours between the public schools and community colleges would be excellent in terms of developing quality sequence for students in mathematics, and other academic and non-academic areas when progressing from the secondary to the higher education levels of instruction. With cooperatively developed goals, faculty may assist students to achieve more optimally. The identified goals should represent the best thinking of involved academicians and instructor/ teachers within the framework of a planned series of meetings arranged to achieve salient objectives. Proper articulation and sequence between secondary and higher education levels of instruction has been minimised too frequently. Conscientious efforts should be inherent to remedy this situation.

Schertz (1993) describes an effort to internationalise Illinois Community College at Peoria with funds a successful written federal grant. A workshop resulted in which involved faculty developed courses pertaining to third world cultures. Three new courses resulted: China, Meso-America, and West Africa. There were challenges involved in achieving the goal of these developed courses. These include influencing the dean on the importance of these courses; having adequate faculty in designing the new courses; money for staff development, and securing college moneys for the new courses.

Ediger (1988) presents a model for conducting a workshop. The first step should involve establishing a theme. Ideally all members of the workshop need to assist in choosing a theme. There must be adequate human, reading material, and audiovisual aids available for the workshop. The rest of the workshop needs to be flexible and open ended. All participants participate in the general session. Here, the members select relevant problem areas to solve. Careful deliberation is necessary so that vital problem area are chosen. Participants need to perceive purpose in each. The problems may pertain to adopting new courses or modifying course content. Objectives in the curriculum may be selected, revised, or deleted. New assessment procedures may be explored and studied.

Within this workshop, participants may volunteer to work on a problem with the goal being to offer viable solutions. Here resources and reference materials should be used. Each committee need to provide progress reports to the other committees. This can be done with printed documents or oral reports. Participants should volunteer to serve on the committee which possesses the most perceived purpose. Beyond the general session and committee endeavours, individuals projects and activities become salient. Each participant has a selected problem to solve or an area of interest to pursue. The individual may wish to share findings with others. Workshops can be an excellent way of opening doors for open communication and the solving of problems.

Divisional meetings are and can be quality ways of improving the curriculum and offer inservice education. An agenda should be available prior to each meeting. Participants should have ample opportunities to study and analyse agenda items, prior to the workshop. Improved quality in interaction among division members is possible when members have time to think through and come up with ideas for change in the curriculum. Each faculty member should have chances to submit items from the agenda. Important agenda items should be covered only, not trivia. Committees, as needed, may be arranged to work on problems, designed by all faculty in the divisional meeting. Ideally, members should serve on the committee which has the most perceived purpose for the participant. A high degree of purpose involved in working on a committee makes for increased energy levels as well as for desiring to carry the work forward until necessary solutions to problems are agreed upon. Reference and resources should be available to assist participants to grow, develop, and achieve. Divisional meetings have as their goal the improvement of the community college curriculum. All items discussed within a committee or the division as a whole must guide participants to become increasingly professional in their duties and responsibilities. (Ediger 1995).

Marlene Cohen (1992) discusses changes that were implemented in Prince George's Community College in Maryland after the results of a survey of 149 of its adjunct faculty members. These changes included the offering of orientation sessions each semester for new faculty members as well as have more faculty workshops. The survey results also indicated developing a handbook for adjunct faculty and honouring an adjunct faculty member each year for outstanding work.

Greive and France (1992) present guidelines in conducting a workshop for new and experienced adjunct faculty. These guidelines resulted in a manual containing workshop and college information, instructional concerns, student traits and concerns, and characteristics of good teaching, among other items.

Kelly (1991-1992) describes an inservice education programme for adjunct faculty on teaching adult learners at Fullerton College in California. The faculty involved experienced discussions and implementation of new teaching methods. Pertaining to questionnaire results from students of the implemented ideas of instruction, the involved students felt an excess amount of time was required for completing course work. There was need to guide adult evening students in time management, according to questionnaire results. Students did feel positive toward the courses, teachers, and methods of instruction used.

There is a need to stress inservice education for all community college instructors. The curriculum offered to students needs to be analysed continuously with needed modifications and changes made. The objectives of instruction need scrutinising in terms of being relevant, salient, and vital. Rational balance should be made in stressing knowledge, skills, and attitudinal ends of instruction.

Learning opportunities for students to attain objectives should stress a multimedia approach such as using textbooks, audio-visual aids, library resources, reference personnel, and independent studies. Quality sequence of learning opportunities is a must so that each student might attain more optimally.

Appraisal of student achievement should analyse if students have achieved the stated goals of instruction. Evaluative procedures may include instructor written tests (multiple choice, true-false, matching, completion/short answer, and essay). Additional techniques of evaluation might well involve anecdotal records, checklists, rating scales, case studies, discussions, and journal writing. Portfolios have become increasingly important in the evaluative process. The portfolio contains a representative sampling of student course work which may be shown to potential employees upon being interviewed.

Additional Methods of Inservice Education

There are numerous other means of emphasising faculty development. Thus, faculty individually may video tape their own teaching performance. The video taped performance is then available for an involved peer to assist in appraising actual teaching and learning. The peer chosen to appraise should be one that the instructor who did the actual teaching on video tape feels comfortable with. An agreed upon set of standards can be emphasised in appraising the video taped teaching. The following appear to be salient standards:

1. Do students in class appear to understand and attach meaning to what is being taught?
2. Is the lesson presentation paced at a speed which is conducive to student learning?
3. Does the instructor sequence or order learning activities which optimise student learning?
4. Do students raise relevant questions and offer vital comments directly related to the ongoing presentation?
5. Are students motivated to achieve and attain?
6. Does the instructor use a variety of learning activities so that students maintain interest in learning? A multimedia approach should be emphasised?

7. Do students receive worthwhile feedback from test and other evaluative results?
8. Is the instructor stressing diverse methodology of instruction to encourage active involvement by students such as using inductive teaching, problem solving, creative and critical thinking, and discovery methods of learning?
9. Does the instructor take time to guide students to perceive purpose in learning?
10. Do students provide feedback to the instructor on the quality of instruction being offered? A checklist or rating scale may be devised by instructors and used by students to evaluate different facets of instruction.

There are numerous means of improving instruction through video taping an instructor's teaching and evaluating the results there from. Improved instruction should be an end result. More than one peer could also assist in appraising the quality of instruction.

Community college instructors might visit the classroom of others who are known to do an excellent job of teaching students. It is good if different community colleges in an area could arrange times for instructors to observe high quality models of instruction. The instructional sites chosen as models must have teaching which emulates the best in community college teaching. Following the observational visit, the instructor and the observer should discuss and analyse what transpired in an ongoing lesson. The observer should discuss with the instructor what may be implemented in the former's instructional situation. An improved curriculum for students should be an end result. Pirozzoli (1993) emphasised that in an age of accountability, better prepared students are expected from higher education graduates. The experiences of the student are an important area of restructuring the curriculum.

In addition to visiting an excellent model of teaching in a community college, instructor may view video tapes of community college instruction. The video tape may be produced locally or ordered from a publishing company. Here, several instructors might observe the video tape and critique the observations made in terms of quality standards. The standards might have been developed from faculty research involving what good teaching is in the community college. Each participant may discuss what can be used in his/her classroom from the observations made. Recommendations should also be made on how to improve teaching-learning situations that need change, as observed from the video tape.

A video tape on retraining displaced workers might well provide excellent content in times of job losses and retrenchment in the economic world. Bogaty et. al. (1984) emphasise that community colleges may play a leading role in retaining workers. In their detailed report, they recommended seven elements be included in worker retraining programmes, including applied learning, technology use, cooperative learning, integration of course content, team teaching, learning labs, an adequate integrated student services.

In Conclusion

Community colleges need to keep abreast of the latest positive trends to offer a quality curriculum for all students. Phelps (1994) wrote the following:

Determining how the nations nearly 1,300 community colleges should proceed toward the 21st century need not be an overwhelming task if we begin using new and improved methods of selecting data to build a more cogent case for what we need to do. We need techniques to demonstrate quality, accountability, and outcomes that are easily discernible and readily available to the various public involved, and above all, we must be willing to communicate with our various publics.

Whether addressing the economy, the welfare system, education, the health care crisis, or crime and violence in our cities, people on the local level are going to have to play an ever greater role in solving the complex problems not only of our cities, but of our suburbs and rural communities as well.

Trends in teaching that need continual addressing include the following:

1. Teaching in the Community College needs to be transformed through the use of technology in its fullest dimensions (Doucette 1994).
2. Interactive Media and its uses should assist learners in community colleges to achieve vital objectives in the curriculum (Sheponik, 1995).
3. Multicultural educational needs incorporation and be updated continuously (Stoll 1994-95).
4. Transformational quality and leadership are musts in the community college curriculum (Harris April, May 1995).
5. Quality instruction and assistance for college students with disabilities need to be incorporated in the community college curriculum (Van Biervliet and Parette 267-273).

REFERENCES

Cohen, Arthur H. *"General Education in Community College,"*. Los Angeles, California, ERIC Clearing House for Community Colleges, 1993.

Cohen, Don (Editor), *"Standards for Curriculum and Pedagogical Reforms Two Year and Lower Division Mathematics."* New York: American Mathematical Association of Two Year Colleges, 1993.

Brunerm Jerome S. *Toward a Theory of Instruction*, Cambridge, Massachusetts: Harvard University Press, 1968.

Doucette, Don (1994), *Transforming and Learning Using Information Technology: A Report From the Field.* Community College Journal, 65, 18-26.

Harris, Zelema (1995), A Journey Worth Taking: Transformational Quality and Leadership. *Community College Journal*. 65, 32-38.

Phelps, Donald (1994). What Lies Ahead for Community College As We Hurdle Toward the 21st Century? *Community College Journal*, 65, 22-25.

National Council Teachers of Mathematics. *Curriculum and Evaluation Standards for Schools*. Reston, Virginia: National Council Teachers of Mathematics, 1989.

Scheponik, Peter, Interactive Multimedia: Challenge, Change and Choice. *Community College Journal*, 65, 20-26.

Schertz, Leanne, "In the 90's: Administrative, Faculty, and Student Perspectives". Paper Presented at the National Midwest Regional Conferences on English in the Two Year College, Madison, Wisconsin, 1993.

Stoll, Marsal. What is Multicultural Education? *Community College Journal*, 65, 10-16.

Ediger, Marlow, *The Curriculum*, Kirksville, Missouri: Simpson Publishing Company, 1988.

Ediger, Marlow, *Relevancy in Elementary Curriculum*. Kirksville, Missouri: Simpson Publishing Company, 1995.

Cohen, Marlene, "Benefits on a Budget: Addressing Adjunct Needs." Paper Presented at the 78th Annual Meeting of the Speech Communication Association. Chicago, Illinois, October 29-November 1, 1992.

Greive, Donand and Richard France, "Orientation to Teaching for Adjunct Faculty." Paper Presented at the National Conference on Successful College Teaching and Administration. Orlano. Florida, March 1-4, 1992.

Kelly, Diana K. *Part Time and Evening Faculty: Promoting Teaching Excellence for Adult and Evening College Students, 1991-1992 Fund for Instructional Improvement Grant Project,* Final Project. Fullerton, California: Fullerton, California, 1992.

Pirozzoli, Don, Restructuring Student Experiences Using Teach Prep Mapping to Integrate Vocational and Academic Curricula.' Paper Presented at the Summer Institute on Institutional Effectiveness and Student Success, Madison, Wisconsin, June 21, 1993.

Van Biervliet, Alan and Howard Parette, Jr. (1994). Teaching Americans with Disabilities Act (ADA) Self Advocacy Skills for College Students. *College Student Journal*, 28, 267-273.

3

Faculty Decision Making in the Community College

Faculty members tend to serve on numerous committees in higher education. There needs to be quality interaction among participants when deliberating and engaging in the solving of problems. I have observed a division meeting in which one person nominated an individual for each of the following positions:

1. representative to the graduate council;
2. representative to the undergraduate council;
3. representative to the faculty senate;
4. representative to the instructional service committee.

In making the nominations, the custom was in the division for the first nomiation for each position to be accepted by unanimous acclimation. In sequence then, a nomination was made, seconded, and accepted by unanimous acclimation. When the final slate of members for each of the above named four committees was accepted and voted upon, one person in the division had made all of the decisions. The voting by unanimous acclimation was done for each position separately, followed by the next nomination in sequence, so that it was not as obvious that a single faculty member had chosen who should fill each position. The minutes of the divisional meeting indicated it was a faculty or divisional decisions that had been made. There are definite recommendations that may be made to improve faculty decision making. The balance of this paper will discuss improving the quality of committee endeavours in higher education.

Optimal Involvement by All Participants

Each member of a committee should have ample opportunities to participate in the ongoing discussions. The chairperson has an important responsibility in encouraging all to participate. Eye contact is needed by the chairperson with each participant. Looking at a few "key" participants is not adequate. Perhaps these few only participate. Adequate time should be given in the meeting for individuals to think critically and creatively pertaining to the topic and problems at hand. Participants then should reflect upon what has been discussed with a related sequence of ideas for discussion that follows. Digressing form the topic being discussed takes up valuable time which needs to be given to the ideas being considered.

We believe it is excellent if participants notice the flow of the discussion so that ideas circulate within a group and not between selected individuals only. Thus content needs to move from one participant to another, not between chairperson and a participant and then back to the chairperson only or largely. When ideas circulate among committee members, there is better chance for all to participate. A feeling of belonging, not isolation, needs to be felt by each person. Too frequently individuals feel they do not belong and fail to become involved. When individuals do not participate, the quality of decisions may suffer. Then too, it is not a faculty decision if selected members do not contribute for whatever reasons, unless they agree with the motion and trend of the discussion. A committee or group should truly believe the decision made reflects the thinking of all members. The minority here must feel that they had adequate input but there is a majority vote which prevails. A consensus would be better than a vote on a motion. To reach a consensus takes much time and participants need to be willing to speak on the topic until there is agreement on a motion. Participants speak on the topic until the weaknesses and areas of disagreement have been worked out. If agreements fail to come in the discussion, then voting must follow.

There are selected guidelines to follow in committee endeavours which should assist in having faculty arrive at a more democratically arrived session. These include, among others, the following:

1. everyone should participate actively, but not be dogmatic in the discussion;
2. participants should stay on the topic being pursued. This criterion when followed makes for more wise use of participant's time.
3. each should be encouraged to participate. The leader and members of the discussion group should be open to wide participation;
4. no person should dominate the discussion;
5. respect for all is must within the committee.

There should be inservice education for faculty to become quality members in a committee. This could be time and money well spent. A consultant who is reputable could certainly work with faculty on how to become good committee members. A workshop in conducting meetings and being high quality members of committees could be a wise investment by a college or university. Improved faculty participation in group work should be an end result. The workshop should provide practical experiences for participants. It should not be a workshop *about* conducting faculty meetings, but rather utilitarian experiences are desired. There are difficulties involved in using what has been learned if a workshop emphasises *about* rather than the actual faculty meeting to bring improvement in the quality of committee endeavours. Administrators should attend the workshop since they may be providing leadership in guiding faculty committee work. In too many cases, administrators find it difficult to let faculty make decisions that are truly democratic. Skills are lacking here in providing needed leadership.

Eliminating Weaknesses

We perceive numerous problems that need to be overcome before committees can function effectively. Cliques may dominate a committee. They have agreed upon their agenda prior to the meeting on what the outcomes should be. Cliques have a very difficult time to accept others and their ideas in committee sessions. The outcomes of a meeting then may not represent the thinking of the committee, but reflects what the clique desires. The minutes of the meetings sent to other faculty may make it appear as if democratically arrived at solutions to problems have been arrived at. Perhaps it is best if cliques are not on the same committee. Not all cliques, of course, would be closely knit so that the thinking of outsiders is not welcomed in a committee setting.

A second problem I perceive is that selected committee members have become quite shrewd in manipulating others and thus hinder active participation by individuals. For example, I have noticed situations such as the following when a committee member says something to manipulate other on the committee:

(a) "We do not have time for that now." This is said by a committee member who may find much time for random talk, but cuts a presenter off from further participation that is very directly related to what is being discussed.

(b) "You have strayed from the topic which we need to get back to." This is said even though the subject matter presented is related to what was being said.

(c) "Lets not repeat what has been said previously." It may be necessary to repeat to clarify ideas or bring committee members back to the topic being pursued. Or, the person making the critical remark may not want to have the contributor receive credit for excellent suggestions made.

(d) "Lets quit beating a dead horse." This remark is made to prevent further discussion on an idea, unless there truly has been repetitious statements.

We believe a committee should be knowledgeable about techniques to manipulate and work in the direction of avoiding these kinds of situations. Why is this important? I want the best conclusions to come from a committee in which all have ownership therein. Thus it behooves committee member to include all in the decision making process. If at all possible, each committee meeting should be videotaped and analysed by participants. We have heard numerous participants express evaluative statements when appraising their own performance in a playback of the video-tape. Comments such as the following have been made:

1. I felt that I did not allow others to participate as much as should have been done. I interrupted too many times when others were speaking in the committee.
2. I was sorry that I cut off a person when more time should have been given to that person making a contribution.
3. I did not face all participants when discussing. It seems as if I was only talking to a few people.
4. I need to speak in complete sentences, rather than sentences fragments.
5. I sounded as if I was irritated at a comment made by a participant. I will need to try harder not to do this.

Poor rapport selected committee members can certainly hinder quality participation. Faculty members should always try to establish good rapport with others from the day they are employed in an institution of higher education. Too frequently, there are faculty members who never speak to each other. It hinders interaction among individuals so that learning from others is not possible. Here again. I believe is an area for inservice education. A university should have as a major goal whereby individuals communicate effectively with others and accept people with diverse attitudes, beliefs, and cultures. One of my criticisms of university administrators is that they lack the skills to work well with different value systems of people who truly think differently. Administrators in higher education need to be able to work with diverse personalities since they are in leadership roles. Faculty desire to have leaders who represent all members, not a sacred few. Too frequently, administrators choose a few to work with and the rest are not valued in discussion settings. For the latter, the self concept suffers and, no doubt, the quality of instruction and interaction among faculty members goes downhill. Acceptance and respect are a two way process between and among faculty and administrators. The best curriculum for students must be developed. This can only be done when administrators and faculty work comparatively to solve problems.

Power Structure in Higher Education

As is always the case in organisations, there is a power structure involved in higher education. We would hope that expert power would be prized highly in the university setting. With expert power, the knowledgeable person possessing needed skills and attitudes is looked up to for guidance and direction. Then too, all participants in committee settings should develop expert power. An agenda, well prepared, prior to any meeting, assists individuals to study, analyse, and reflect upon what will be discussed. An unprepared person can not attain expert power in a committee setting. One of the authors recently sat in on a committee for a national organisation in education in which the packet of materials, containing forty three pages, was handed out at the meeting which meets once a year. There was no way one could read that many pages at the meeting. Most committee members were then ill prepared for the three hour meeting. Better it would be if these materials had been mailed to committee members several weeks ahead of the national convention. We felt left out due to this being my first attendance as a member of this committee. There were two former presidents of the national organisation as members of the committee who seemingly possessed expert power in making necessary decisions. However, the rest of the membership was not able to participate adequately. Each person then should have ample opportunities to attain expert power.

A person may be weak in deliberations within a committee due to the content in the discussion being completely outside of his/her area of expertise. For example, a modified degree programme being considered in sociology without the assistance of instructors in sociology at the meeting makes for a lack of expert power. Instructors in sociology here must definitely assist others in making quality decisions. They become resource persons for others on the committee. Committee members need to have ample opportunities to understand and attach meeting to proposals presented within a group setting.

Let us consider other sources of power. Delegated authority, such as an administrator whose professional job description emphasises a leadership position, certain has a vital role to play in developing committee competence. Administrators can influence decision making much due to their designated status. He/she should assist in releasing the creative skills and abilities of faculty. It is difficult in being a good leader in the educational arena. Faculty members desire leadership, but not coercion. Faculty wish to be involved in decision making which personally affects what they will be doing in terms of professional responsibilities. Administrators need to be careful in having undue power in committee decision making due to their designated role in higher education. They should facilitate quality discussions and encourage active participation by participants. Expert power is a key concept for administrators to stress in committee work. Acceptance of all faculty members is a must for university administrators. Administrators should be expert in conducting committee work. They need to have an inward desire to improve the quality of decision making. A relaxed environment should be in the offing when discussions are being conducted in a committee setting.

There are additional sources of power in the university setting and that is charismatic power. Persons of charisma possess social graces, charm, and radiance. They tend to be liked by many power in society. It would be good to have a blend of expert and charismatic power in human beings. Individuals tend to look up to charismatic people for leadership and guidance. However, expert power must come first when considering a power base in faculty meetings. A charismatic person may influence and do this readily, but one wants the best ideas possible as a result of committee endeavours. That is why expert power becomes so important. To have an excellent university curriculum, committee members need to be highly knowledgeable, skillful, and possess positive attitudes.

Beyond expert, designated, and chatrismatic powers, there is authoritarian power. Actually, authoritarian power can be present in any of the previously mentioned three kinds of power. For purposes of discussion and evaluation, lets us consider it separately. The authoritarian individual desires to have a on street of communication. Thus the communication moves from the authoritarian person to others in a committee setting. He/she wishes to have followers only, not creative minds. An authoritarian person with designated status could have much negative influence in a committee setting. It behooves a designated person, such as a university administrator, to work in the direction of achieving harmonious relationships with faculty and emphasising quality in the decision making arena. With video-taping of committee meetings, it is quite easy to identify the person who is dogmatic and dictatorial. Evaluating the results of the videotape can aid participants to assess each contribution made in terms of assisting the group to becoming increasingly democratic. Inservice growth in the university arena is a necessity if valid decisions are to be made on the committee level.

Acceptance of Others

How can committee function so that all are accepted and respected? What can be done to avoid rejection and a lack of harmony? Faculty members who do not speak to each other lose out on acquiring knowledge due to a lack of interaction. One can learn much from and by listening to other individuals. This is true if it is within or outside of committee endeavours. When university faculty retire, one item that is missed by many is the lack of opportunities to interact with other professionals in the academic world. We have heard many retirees say this. Thus there is joy in orally communicating with colleagues. It becomes uncomfortable emotionally if there is mistrust among faculty. There also is difficulty in carrying out the necessary functions of university personnel if disharmony and petty jealously are in evidence.

For positive interactions to accrue, faculty members should assist each other to achieve feelings of belonging. In committee work, individuals desire to feel they belong. Belonging to a group develops committee cohesiveness. Opportunities then increase when emphasising group dynamics. With quality group dynamics involved, a committee moves forward toward harmonious goal attainment. This does not eliminate or minimise feelings of creativity. Within the framework of respect toward others, committee members need to express unique ideas and yet reach group consensus through discussions. Creativity is necessary so that the best ideas possible come from committee members. New ideas are needed from participants in committees so that the best curriculum possible is available for university students. Ideas are modified as they are considered and reflected upon. Additional contributions by faculty assist in the modification process. New ideas presented tend to stress cognitive dissonance within individuals. Thus what was formerly adhered to needs changing due to a lack of congruence with previously held ideas. Feelings of belonging then aid the committee member to feel comfortable in presenting unique ideas in the committee setting.

In addition to developing feelings of belonging, individuals also desire self esteem. Thus a person wishes to be recognised for accomplishments and contributions made. Talents and abilities of individuals should always be recognised. If they are not recognised, other committee members lose out on strengths to make better decisions. Feelings of antagonism toward contributions of others hinders committee progress. We want the best decisions possible form committee members. This can only be possible if strengths (expert power) of individuals are used. One should give credit where credit is due. Positive reinforcement is then in evidence.

Security needs are salient for faculty to experience. Too many changes can be emphasised at one time or over a period of time. It is good to make changes when there is a need to do so, after diagnosis has been emphasised. Faculty and administration must make changes when necessary in different facets of the university curriculum. Otherwise a university can become an outdated and outmoded institution. But to emphasise and implement modifications and restructuring continuously make for situations in which faculty may well develop feelings of insecurity. To do well in the instructional and committee arenas, there needs to be a certain amount of stability. Thus a balance needs to exist between change and stability in the university curriculum. This balance must be felt by the university community.

With belonging, esteem, and security needs met, the chances are that faculty will be better able to acquire knowledge and skills, resulting in an improved curriculum for faculty, administrators, and students. To achieve optimally for all certainly is a quality goal for the university community to attain.

In Conclusion

Faculty members should be involved in decision making in which the outcomes here are truly those that have been arrived at in a democratic manner. Each committee member then has had adequate input into the final decision, arrived at by the involved committee. Negative comments made toward the contributions of others must be eliminated. Comments such as these hinder communication; the best decisions are not arrived at when positive statements are lacking. Respect and acceptance if all committee members is a must. Feelings of belonging, esteem, and security should be inherent on the part of participants when working in a committee setting. These feelings assist faculty in achieving more optimally.

Expert power needs to be accepted in a committee setting. Charismatic power is desirable if coupled with expert power. Authoritative power should definitely be minimised or eliminated. Designates power involving administrators should stress expert power in decision making. The university community should function in an optimal manner so that students experience the best curriculum possible.

4

Community College Curriculum Development

The community college curriculum needs continuous evaluation to notice necessary changes and modifications which should be made. The societal arena does not remain stable, but appears to experience rather continuous transformations. Faculty and administrators need to address needed alterations which may improve the curriculum. Which areas need to be viewed for possible changes?

Objectives of instruction from each instructor should be studied, analysed, and updated. There are diverse categories of objectives in the curriculum. Knowledge objectives, including relevant facts, concepts, and generalisations, might need updating as evidence warrants. Second, skills objectives emphasise using acquired knowledge. These skills might well include critical and creative thinking as well as problem solving. Thus higher levels of cognition are being emphasised in teaching and learning. It is vital that the level of application is in the repertoire of the community college student as a result of having met graduation standards. Applying what has been acquired may well mean to guide learners to perceive that what is presented in a lesson is related to that which was previously learned. This will assist students to retain content learned and find it useful in the college and societal setting. Knowledge objectives then should not be separated from skills ends since the latter emphasises using the former.

A third category which community college faculty and administrators need to evaluate are affective goals. The affective goals stress that students achieve positive feelings toward knowledge and skills acquired. If negative attitudes are in the repertoire of the student, the chances are that future as well as present learning will not occur sequentially. With good attitudes, students learn to appreciate, grow, develop, and feel in positive manner toward knowledge and skills. Thus quality affect is an outcome of each lesson and unit taught by the instructor. Community college instructors need to work in the direction of guiding students to learn to like diverse curriculum areas that contain the goals of instruction.

The Community College Curriculum

An important issue in the community college curriculum pertains to integrating vocational and general education. In a survey of 295 community colleges (USA), randomly selected, the following were emphasised as means to integrating the vocational and the academic:

1. having general education requirements for students;
2. stressing applied academic courses;
3. bringing in academic skills into the vocational arena;
4. emphasising modules from the academic into vocational courses work;
5. using a multi-disciplinary curriculum by joining together the academic and the vocational;
6. implementing a college within a college approach;
7. advocating English skills and remediation within the framework of the vocational.

Major hindrances in moving toward the above criteria included the status differences between instructors in the academic as compared to vocational realm of instruction as well as leadership not being in evidence to make these changes. (29 and Kraskouskas, 1992).

There are numerous barriers to change and innovation in community colleges. Among others, these may include complex campus procedures in working toward revision, state mandates which need fulfilment, tradition as a goal of the institution and of instructors, work inherent in restructuring the curriculum, fear of the unknown by instructors and administrators, a do not fix it philosophy when all is going smoothly, a lack of skills for instructors and administrators in working together in committee setting to emphasise planned change, a need for change agents to move the curriculum from where it is to where it should be, beliefs by faculty and administration that the community college curriculum as it does not restructuring, and complacency by those involve in shaping needed changes.

Pautler (1992) emphasises changes that community colleges face. These will require skills in leaders for those planning needed changes. Leadership provides the opportunity for innovation to faculty, as well as the need for making ongoing curricular changes as situations arise. Planning should be sequential and continuous.

Too frequently, instructors and administrators lack vision in restructuring the curriculum. Planning of the curriculum is necessary and should be done without interruption. Changes are not made for the sake of doing so, but rather for the sake of improving the curriculum for students. As society and its requirements change, so must the community college curriculum evaluate what is presently being offered to students and make necessary modifications. Trends in society need careful study to determine objectives, course content, and evaluation procedures in the curriculum. Collaboration of faculty, administrators, students, and interested lay persons is of vital importance so that the goals of learners are being met. A work force is needed in society which will be increasingly productive in diverse endeavours. Thus community colleges need to offer students the best curriculum possible. Students individually should attain as optimally as possible.

Arnold (1992) advocates that employers develop high tech positions which pay well. Community colleges need to train and education students well so that efficiency on the job is in evidence. There needs to be linkage among k-12, post secondary education, and the world of work. The Secretary's Commission on Achieving Necessary Skills (SCANS) emphasises skills that should be taught in education and at the work place. These include the following:

1. planning in using resources, knowledge and information skills, applying technology skills, and working effectively with others;
2. assisting employers to recruit and train workers who can do well in the world of work;
3. motivating workers to achieve well at the work place;
4. preparing workers for the 21st century.

There are indeed may expectations from workers in high tech positions. Society has become quite complex. Thus workers need to be able to identify and solve problems. This requires being able to use reference sources directly related to the problems being pursued. Solutions to problems generally are tentative and require testing in the work place. Cooperative problem solving will be stressed. Individuals then need to be able to work well with others. Hostility and anger toward others has no place in achieving goals: These feelings hinder cooperative endeavours in achieving necessary objectives of the business or company. It is of utmost importance to secure the most capable individuals as a beginning step in developing a competent work force. These workers must be sought and encouraged to work in the market place. People with high energy levels tend to attain goals more effectively as compared to the unmotivated. Inservice growth and development will then be used in a more effective manner. Quality workers should be in evidence presently as well as for the next century. Highly motivated people who have an inward desire to learn and to achieve are a credit and an asset to the business and place of work.

Academic course work is viewed as being much more superior as compared to vocational tracks. This is indeed unfortunate. There are high school students who cannot benefit from a heavy dose of the academic. They are more inclined to like vocational and technical course work. One should not view it to be segregation when secondary school students go the occupational route of studies. Marmaras (1992) describes a partnership programme between a high school of Warwick. Rhode Island and the nearby Rhode Island Community College (RICC). Secondary students are evaluated in grade ten to participate in the cooperative programme. In grade eleven, students start their work in fields such as to pursue a career in a technological, business, or health field. After satisfactory completion of the eleventh grade, students may then enter any technical programme at RICC.

The cooperative Warwick high school and RICC may and could solve many problems in education. Certainly students might perceive increased purpose or reasons for learning when pursuing what is of interest to them personally. Too frequently, secondary educators place a very high value on the academic areas of learning solely. But what happens if learners do not wish that kind of a curriculum? I have known a high school student who received low grades in academic course work, but became a successful contractor. As contractors in the practical world, they placed numerous estimates for building buildings for others. Mathematics then became useful and functional. Many of these individuals as high school students did not care for the study of literature due to "possessing poor reading skills." And yet, these same individuals as adults read complex manuals for installing air conditioners, centralised heating units, and other modern devices. I truly believe we have not met the needs of these students when the demand is made to excel in the academic areas largely. If educators fear that segregation is involved with an academic track or a separate vocational track in the secondary school, perhaps a cooperative arrangement can be worked out between a high school and a nearby community college. The cooperative agreement would emphasise that high school students could spend part or all of their time in the community college studying for a career. A cooperative agreement might spell out the objectives that a student is to achieve and how each objective is to be attained. Certainly, students should understand how they are to be appraised to notice success in the cooperatively arranged programme. Students then are learning technical and vocational skills in preparation for the world of work with a satisfying career. The academics are not eliminated but students acquire applied academic knowledge with major emphasis being placed upon getting ready for being in the work place. The work place should be a satisfying situation for the individual, not a place to dread. Remuneration for services preformd must be adequate so that a quality life style may be in evidence.

Ethics is a key concept to emphasise in the community college and in the real world of work. In fact, ethics should be inherent in whatever is done, at any accountable age level. Engelhardt (1993) describes a course in ethics that sophomores take at the Utah Valley Community College at Orem. The interdisciplinary course is entitled "Ethics and Values" and emphasises the following strands— duties, rights, utility, sexual morality, abortion, euthanasia, nuclear war, and capital punishment.

All persons should experience discussions pertaining to ethics, be it in course of work or in informal settings. With rampant crime, immortality, and corruption, it behooves instructors and others to assist learners to attain a set of ethical standards and values that truly provide direction in life and living. The consequences of numerous acts may indeed be highly detrimental to individuals. In addition to crime, immorality, and corruption, there are many other avenues in life which violate proper standards for ethics and values. The latter include items such as rudeness, biases, hatreds and dislike toward others, as well as theft of minor items from the work place where the cases of detection are small indeed. Appropriate ethics and values emphasise that one accepts and treats others with respect. One is honest and sincere in dealing with human beings and is humane toward animals.

The Educational Policies Commission of the National Education Association (1962) in their booklet entitled *The Central Purpose of American Education* stated "The purpose which runs through and strengthens all other purposes—the common thread of education—is the development of the ability to think." Here are selected experts from their booklet:

1. Whenever an objective has been judged desirable for the individual or the society, it is tended to be accepted as a valid concern of the school.
2. The basic American value—respect for the individual, has led to one of the major changes which the American people have placed on their schools; to foster that development of the individual capacities which will enable human being to become the best person capable of becoming.
3. The free person has a rational grasp of himself/herself, the surroundings, and the relationship between them.
4. The cultivated powers of the mind have always been basic in achieving freedom. The powers involve the processes for recalling and imagining, classifying and generalising, comparing and evaluating, analysing and synthesising, and deducting and inferring. These processes enable one to apply logic and the available evidence to his/her ideas, actions, and pursue better whatever goals he/she may have. This is not to say that the rational powers are all of the life or all of the mind, but they are of the essence of the ability to think.

Earlier, (1938), the Educational Policies Commission (EPC) listed four major goal strands of education. These were a description of the educated person, the educated member of a family, the educated producer and consumer, and the educated citizen. Inside these four strands are numerous objectives that emphasise developing ethical character.

Still earlier, the National Education Association (NEA) in 1918 came out with the Seven Cardinal Principles of Education. One of the seven was to develop within students the skills and abilities of achieving ethical character. Thus the development of ethical character has been a goal for student attainment through the decades and still remains vital.

Ethics education and application should be a definite goal of the community college curriculum. Increased peace of mind and character is an end result of behaving ethically. Students need to apprise the self in terms of criteria stressing the ethical being. Throughout the work experience of students and adults, emphasis should be placed upon development of ethical behaviour in the community college curriculum as well as in the curriculum of life.

Hart and Boehm (1992) describes programmes of community college Education for intellectually handicapped individuals. They discuss the philosophy of eliminating barriers for handicapped individuals and a commitment to assist these persons in job training. Further, the curricula content, admission requirements, and funding for the programme are discussed. Reading and writing skills are not required as entry goals to these community colleges in Canada. Handicapped individuals must have an employment goal as well as support from a legal guardian. They will develop skills in class participation, social skills, and orientation to the work place.

It is vital that community colleges have salient understandings, skills, and attitudinal goal for all students to attain. To achieve these objectives, students should experience work place skills to achieve objectives. Evaluation, using a variety of approaches, should be emphasised to ascertain of the stated objectives have been attained by learners. A gradual transition should be in evidence to guide students to enter the work force after completing community college requirements.

Principles of Teaching and Learning in Community Colleges

There are definite principles of learning that community college instructors should stress. Thus instructors should guide students to perceive the relationships of newly presented content with what learners acquired in prior times. Content that is related will be retained longer than that which is unrelated. Then too, it is easier to apply content to new situations if a relationship of ideas is perceived. Second, students need to understand what was thought and attach necessary meanings to these items of knowledge, skills, and attitudes.

Meaning theory is important for instructors to emphasise when teaching students. Third, students need guidance to perceive purpose in learning. With purpose, there are accepted reasons by students for learning and achieving. Best it is if a student learns due to intrinsic motivation. Thus within the learner there is a desire to learn, interest might be a factor, among others. Extrinsic motivation emphasises that a student learns due to something outside the actual learning of content that motivates, such as a high grade or a test that is forthcoming. The rewards then motivate and encourage learning. We believe that lifelong learning is best facilitated through intrinsic motivation. The student then has a high energy level for learning due to personal factors that relate to the subject matter or skills being studied. If a student lacks motivation, he/she will not attend to what is being taught and will not remember that which emphasised in ongoing lessons and units of study. Perhaps, there was little intent to listen to or hear what was presented by the community college instructor.

The instructor can do much to motivate students. One way is to present subject matter in an interesting way. There are numerous methods of instruction that may be used. The method chosen should harmonise with the learning styles of involved students. An inductive procedure of instruction stresses the use of many questions issued by the instructor. Answers which come form students assist them to achieve vital concepts and generalisations. With a deductive approach, the instructor lectures in a stimulating manner and then evaluates how much students have learned and how much they can apply in a new situation. Through the use of tests and discussions, among others means, the instructor may ascertain how much students have acquired from content presented deductively. The instructor may also wish to emphasise a problem solving approach in teaching-learning situations. Here, students need to be stimulated to identify vital problems within a lecture, discussion, or audio-visual presentation, among other learning activities. After the problem(s) have been identified, students may work individually or within a committee setting to locate needed information in answer to the stated problem area(s).

Diverse reference sources, reading and nonreading activities, might be used in securing needed information in answer to the problem. An hypothesis is developed directly related to the identified problem(s). After thought, deliberation, critical and creative thinking, the hypothesis is accepted, refuted, or modified, inductive, deductive, and problem solving procedures may be emphasised in the academic as well as in vocational training. The word "subject matter" or "content" as used by the writer emphasises knowledge and skills developed or acquired to solve problems. Problems solving has many uses in that this approach may be used in community college course work as well as in the societal arena.

Tuckman (1995) has done much research on developing an interpersonal teaching model. He developed the Tuckman Teacher Feedback Form (TTFF). Students are to place to check mark in the space the best describes his/her teacher. The check mark is placed in one of the seven boxes (a seven point scale) pertaining to each trait on the TTFF form. The following traits, among others, then are evaluated by each student pertaining to the teacher experienced:

1.	Disorganised	Organised
2.	Clear	Unclear
3.	Aggressive	Soft spoken
4.	Confident	Uncertain
5.	Common place	Clever
6.	Creative	Ordinary
7.	Old-fashioned	Modern
8.	Likable	"Stuck Up"
9.	Exciting	Boring
10.	Sensitive	Rough

In between each pair of words such as number one above (Disorganised Organised), there are seven boxes for making one check mark. These boxes are labeled. 1. Very; 2. Somewhat; 3. A Bit; 4. In the Middle; 5. A Bit; 6. Somewhat; 7. Very.

Certainly teachers who care, accept others, reveal warmth, are creative, and are likable should have a more positive influence on students than those who reveal opposite traits in working with others. Interpersonal instructional skills are needed by community college instructors to guide optimal student achievement.

In Closing

Community college instructors need to plan the best objective, learning activities for students to attain the stated objectives, and appraisal procedures possible so that graduating students are ready for the work place. These graduates need to be prepared for the challenges of a changing society. Updated training will be necessary in the future for each worker. The work place should have well educated workers who feel challenge to do the best possible in producing quality products and processes. Instructors on the community college level should stress the knowledge, skills, and attitudes which are positive and induct learners into the world of work. Ample room is available in a community college to prepare students who will transfer to a four year institution of higher education. These also need to experience the best of objectives, learning opportunities, and evaluation procedures.

REFERENCES

Grubb, W. and Kraskouskas, Eileen. (1992), "*A Time to Every Purpose: Integrating Occupational and Academic Education in Community Colleges and Technical Institutes*", Berkeley, California: National Centre for Research in Vocational Education.

Pautler, Albert J. (1992), "*Curriculum Leadership, Innovation and Change.*" *Community Junior College Quarterly of Research and Practice*, April-June.

Parker, Arnond (1982), "*An Associate Degree in High Performance Manufacturing.*" *ERIC: Resource in Education.*

Marmaras, Judy and Nari, Pat (1992). "*Tech Prep Associate Degree Programme Guide: Tech Prep Associate Programme, Business Administration Associate Degree Programme, Office of Administration Associate Degree Programme*, Allied Health Associate Degree Programme." Warwick: Community College of Rhode Island.

Englehardt, Elaine Eliason, (1993), *Curriculum Diversity Through a Core Approach to Ethics."* Paper Presented at the International Conference for Community College Chairs, Deans, and other Instructional Leaders, Phoenix, Arizona, February 17-20.

5

Teaching English in the Community College Curriculum

Community college students must experience a curriculum that is perceived as being relevant. With the knowledge and skills explosion in society, students need to feel the objectives being stressed in English have worth presently as well as in the future. Instructors should select each objective carefully in the curriculum. Students must receive the best education possible in a changing society which demands workers having quality knowledge, skills, and attitudes.

Objectives in the English Curriculum

Who should select objectives for students attainment? The instructor of the course may choose all of these ends in the curriculum. Each objective must then have careful scrutiny. The instructor realises that chosen objectives must meet the needs of the learner as well as be important in the societal arena. Trivia, outdated goals, and the transient must be weeded out. There is much to be taught. The irrelevant should not be brought in to teaching-learning situations. The instructor individually then needs to implement objectives that only educate and develop readiness for the societal arena, be it in a job, occupation, or future profession.

Much is written and discussed or higher levels of cognition for student learning in the classroom. These higher levels of thought are salient in the academic world as well as in society.

Thus critical thinking must be stressed as an objective by the community college instructor. To think critically, the student should analyse content. Breaking subject matter into component parts and reflecting upon each needs to be emphasised. Comparisons are made between what is known and the new knowledge acquired. Discrepancies are noticed, if in evidence. Statements are challenged as to being logical or harmonising with scientific data. Glittering generalities, bandwagon approaches, overgeneralising, inadequate data to generalise, hasty conclusions drawn, and inadequate examination of content studied should stress analysing of subject matter. Separating facts from opinions, fantasy from reality, and accurate from inaccurate statements further emphasise critical thinking. Critical thinking then is needed to deal with abstract situations as well with the concrete or real world.

A second higher cognitive objective that must be in evidence in teaching-learning situations is creative thinking. Classroom situations and the real world needs original ideas. The tried and true too frequently do not work. Change is a key element in the curriculum and in life's many endeavours. Novel ideas are necessary to come up with the new and the relevant. The community college instructor needs to place major emphasis upon learners thinking creatively in ongoing lessons and units.

Third, problem solving should also receive high priority in the curriculum. Students need guidance in class to identify important problems. A hypothesis or tentative answer to the problem must result. Each hypothesis needs testing, using a variety of reference sources. Textbooks, audio-visual materials, and other reference sources can well be used to test the stated hypothesis. As a result of testing, the hypothesis may need revising. Problem solving activities stimulate students to think since learners are actively involved in the learning process. Students here definitely are not passive recipients of knowledge, but identify and solve problems.

Learning Activities

Students need to experience quality activities to attain objectives. The activities may be chosen solely by the teacher or student-teacher planning can be implemented. If the teacher alone determines the activities, a logical curriculum results in that the teacher orders or sequences experiences for learners. If teacher-student planning is stressed in the curriculum, a psychological curriculum might be an end result due to the latter being involved in ordering his/her experiences. One issue of teaching community college English students pertains to who should be involved in sequencing learning opportunities for students.

A variety of activities need to be in the offing. Variety is necessary to provide for each student. Learners do possess diverse learning styles. Concrete and semiconcrete activities aid some students to achieve more than that in the abstract. For others, the abstract is favoured in teaching-learning situations. Inquiry learning is favoured by some. Whereas, deductive procedures are liked best by others. Student self-selection versus instructor choice of activities and experiences has a long history and needs resolving. If student-instructor planning is used in the English curriculum, a psychological curriculum results in that learners, in part, sequence their own experiences.

Evaluation of Achievement

The instructor needs to use a variety of evaluation techniques to appraise student progress. Attitudes of students toward the course can best be evaluated by the instructor using quality criteria. Thus appraising the interests, feelings, and the affective domain is salient. Quality attitudes toward learning assist students to attain more optimally.

Social development must receive adequate emphasis in the course. Students need to get along well with others in the community college as well as in society. Otherwise participation efforts by students will be hindered. Working harmoniously with other people is necessary so that tasks, jobs, and plans are completed. Much work in society requires social skills since people work together in the societal arena. Cooperation is necessary. Creative beings working well with others is an ideal.

To evaluate social growth, the instructor may note items such as the following, among others, in student classroom committee endeavours:

1. all staying on the topic or project being pursued;
2. no one dominating committee work;
3. each contributing optimally;
4. respect for the thinking of participants in evidence;
5. acceptance of each member being observable.

Cognitive learning is evaluated frequently by instructors. Essay test items may well measure higher levels of cognitive growth in English. Each essay item should be adequately delimited so that students understand what is needed. They should then not be so broadly written that many pages are needed to respond to one essay item, nor should they be so specific in that facts are necessary as responses. Critical and creative thinking as well as problem solving objectives should be emphasised by the English instructor when developing essay test items.

Multiple choice items may be written to ascertain learner progress. The stem of each multiple choice item together with each given response should be grammatically correct. Each response needs to be plausible not ridiculous. Clearly written multiple choice test items have much to recommend themselves to measure learner achievement in English. Multiple choice items should evaluate learners in higher cognitive levels of achievement.

True-false tests may be written by the instructor to appraise student progress. These kinds of test items must be clearly written to eliminate vagueness. Tricky words need to be omitted so that an item is either true or false. If an item is false, the student may cross out the incorrect part and write in what is correct. True-false tests can measure vital subject matter learning. They may be used to appraise student attainment of relevant concepts and generalisations that the instructor deems to be significant.

Completion items have their place in appraising community college student attainment. Relevant content which students should achieve can be measured using completion tests. It is excellent if the instructor uses these kinds of test items to measure significant conclusions and principles in the curriculum which learners should have acquired. The instructor wants to know if the goals of the course have been achieved by students. A variety of procedures of evaluation must then be used. To measure student attainment using completion tests, an adequate amount of content in each test item must be written so that students know what is desired in each blank space in a completion test. For example, the following does not possess adequate content for students to respond to:

— and — are—in the nation of France.

Guesswork only could determine which words to write into the blank spaces. Student achievement is then not being measured in terms of goal attainment. A final kind of test item to measure learner attainment is the matching test. There need to be more responses in one column as compared to the other so that the process of elimination may not be used excessively. If the two columns for matching had the same number of responses, the student may be able to respond to those known first to be correct and then answer many of the unknown correctly with the process of elimination.

Test items need to be valid and reliable. For validity to occur, the student must have had opportunities to learn that which is contained in the test items. Face validity then is being stressed. The instructor writes test items then the students have had opportunities to learn what is contained therein.

Reliability can be emphasised using test-retest, split-half, and/or alternate forms. Consistency of results is important when measuring student progress; otherwise the test may have little value.

Standardised tests are used by some instructors to determine learner progress. These are also called norm-referenced tests. Standardised tests may not measure as carefully the goals of instruction as compared to instructor written tests. They have their values in comparing one's own students with that of the norm group of a standardised test. Standardised tests are much more expensive to use as compared to instructor developed tests since they must be purchased from a publishing company. A community college will require some kind of standardised test be given to all students, such as a predictive test or an achievement test.

In Closing

Community college English instructors need to select each objective carefully for student achievement. Individual objectives must be relevant to the learner and be useful in implementation in the societal arena. Meaning, interest, and purpose must be attached by the student in goal attainment.

Quality sequence should be experienced by learners individually. Students must perceive relationships between the new content presented with that acquired previously.

The instructor needs to be a good evaluator. Diverse procedures of evaluation should be used to determine student progress. Validity and reliability are two concepts that need stress in the appraisal process. Students need to attain optimally in English.

6

Teaching Science in the Community College Curriculum

Science professors in college need to follow definite criteria in the psychology of learning when teaching students. Thus, professors must develop and maintain learner interest. The interests of students is vital if optimal attainment is to accrue. To be interested, the student and the science curriculum become one and not separate entities. A professor then needs to use voice inflection to emphasise that which is salient and important. Proper stress pitch, and juncture in ongoing presentations assist the professor to secure the attention of students. Also, the professor must use a variety of methods of instruction. Variety consists of the use of discussions, experiments, demonstrations, lectures and explanations, videotapes, as well as filmstrips, slides, tapes, and films. Methods of procedure used are geared to having students achieved objectives and goals of instruction. These methods should guide learners to attain as much as possible on an individual basis. In addition to securing the interests of students, the science professor should also guide learners to attach meaning to the ongoing learning opportunities. To attach meaning, the student must understand and comprehend content presented. Memorisation of content is not adequate. Rather, the student needs to put acquired subject matter into his/her own words. When learners realise that language is used to present facts, concepts, and generalisations, they have matured in achieving content and abstract ideas in science. Language is a tool for communication and not an end in and of itself. Within the framework of language, the science professor must guide students to think critically and creatively, as well as to plan and follow through in attaining worthwhile ends.

In addition to interest and meaning, the science professor must assist learners to develop quality attitudes. These needed attitudes consist of being able to stress objectivity in one's investigations and approaches in dealing with scientific phenomena. A desire to learn more and conceive of learning as being lifelong and having no end truly reflects the attitude(s) of scientists. Preserving with the task at hand and not letting up is salient. With persevering, the student in science pursues until goals have been attained. Perceiving gaps in knowledge provides impetus in wanting to narrow or eliminate the gap. Thus an attitude of wanting to know and desiring closure is then in evidence. Quality attitudes guide the student in wanting to achieve optimally in science.

Philosophy of Teaching Science

The professor of teaching science needs to view and understand divers philosophic schools of thought in order to assist each student to attain optimally. A project method may be used in whole or in part. With the project method, the professor encourages each learner in context to select a project to complete. The professor is a stimulator and helper here not a lecturer nor explainer. The student selects the project to complete. The professor provides input as needed in the project method of teaching science. Once the student has chosen a project, he/she then plans how to achieve the purpose of project completion. The planning must be thorough and comprehensive. After its planning, the learner may then actually implement the plans. Here is where the actual work by the student is viewed and sequential steps noticed to achieve closure of the project. Following the completion of the project, evaluation of its quality needs to be in evidence. Criteria of excellence must be used to appraise quality. The professor of science must be available, if at all possible, to give needed help to learners at each step along the way in the project method of instruction. Project methods are quite open ended in terms of a philosophy of teaching. Students are heavily involved in decision making. A project may stress the making of teaching aids in a teaching of science course, developing models of elements making one or more compounds, writing a term paper that investigates a problem area, or giving a report in class that emphasises answering a question identified by learners in the class setting.

Problem solving methods have a little more structure as compared to project means of teaching. In ongoing lessons and units of instruction. A problem is identified. The problem requires data gathering in depth. A variety of reference sources are use to secure the needed data. A hypothesis results. The hypothesis must be clearly stated and is subject to testing. Revision of the tentative hypothesis may be necessary as a result of the test.

Problem solving in experiments and in the laboratory setting might well be the heart of the methods of science. Other materials should also be used to gather data an to check hypothesis such as reading sources and audiovisual methods. Problem solving is a valuable skill in science as well as in life itself. In life, individuals and groups continually select and arrive at situations, usually tentative in nature, to problems. Hypothesis and answers are continually subjected to new experiences with revisions in the offing. Problem solving works well too in all courses that students take be it in the social sciences, languages and literature, mathematics, as well as others. Students continually face the problem of how to study for a test in any course or class being taken. Financing a student's costs of pursuing higher education is becoming an increasingly great problem to solve.

Professors in teaching may use measurably stated objectives in teaching-learning situations. The professor writes these objectives as precisely as possible. There is no guesswork involved in determining what students are to learn when analysing these ends. A student either does or does not attain each objective. The professor may even announce to the class prior to instruction what they are to learn in today's lesson. Learners then have security in knowing what they will be responsible for learning. Students have increased security in realising items that will be on a test, be it criterion referenced or teacher written test items such as true false multiple choice, matching, completion, and/or essay. With measurably stated objectives, the professor or his/her colleagues will come up with the same results when scoring test results. Interscorer reliability is important in that consistency or results should be in the offing when these evaluators score tests of each student. Objectivity is a key concept to stress in scoring tests as well as in determining what will be taught to students when viewing each measurably stated objective in teaching and learning situations. Validity becomes a key concept when harmonising evaluation procedures with the stated objectives. Measuring then is always done in terms of objectives stressed in the science curriculum. What is taught is emphasised within each objective of instruction. Thus the learning activities match up with the objectives as well as the evaluation procedures with the stated objectives. The professor may count the number of objectives attained by each student. Scores on tests may be phrased for each student in terms of percentiles, standard deviations above and below the mean, as well as in quartile deviations. Numerical results are then wanted from students.

As another philosophy, a subject centred science curriculum may be emphasised. The abstract is then preferred to the concrete and semiconcrete in terms of learning activities provided for students. Mind is real and needs to be developed in a subject centred approach in the teaching of science. Mental development of students become primary objective of instruction. Quality attitudes as a goal of instruction may be stressed if they assist to attain more optimally in the knowledge domain.

The professor here needs to emphasise cultivation of the intellect in teaching and learning situations. Higher levels of cognition including critical thinking and analysing of content presented in ongoing lessons and plans of instruction must be stressed. Students then need to achieve vital facts, concepts, and generalisations in the science curriculum. The professor of science instruction must select with great care that which assists learners to develop well intellectually and guides each to inquire worthwhile content.

Heavy learner input in to the science curriculum is still another philosophy of instruction. Here, students may choose what to learn and which to omit in terms of learning activities and experiences. Thus, a learning stations approach may be stressed. The professor then needs to develop stations with four to five tasks at each station. At each station a variety of types of learning opportunities need to be in the offing. Students may also plan with the professor alternative tasks to complete. Time on task is always salient for students when selecting individual or committee endeavours at the diverse stations of instruction. Students should also be involved in appraising their own individual or group performance. Quality criteria must be used to appraise progress. The professor serves as a guide and motivator, not a lecturer. Learners need to assume personal responsible for their progress and achievement. Stations of instruction may be developed by the professor or better yet through professor—student planning.

In Closing

Professors have within their grasp selected guidelines to use in teaching students. From the psychology of learning, professors need to make lessons in science interesting and use a variety of learning activities. Students must perceive meaning in ongoing activities. Purpose in learning is of utmost importance in that learners then accept intrinsic reasons for achieving. Quality attitudes assists students to attain optimally.

Philosophy of instruction provides further guidance to the professor in teaching-learning situations. Each should be used as it assists learners to achieve more optimally. These philosophies include the project method, problem solving, measurably stated objectives, subject centred procedures, and student choice. The professor is the decision-maker as to which philosophy to stress to guide each student to learn as much as possible.

Additional Reading

Bhaskara Rao, Digumarti (1994). *Scientific Aptitude*. New Delhi: Ashish Publishing House. ISBN 81-7024-658-X.

Bhaskara Rao, Digumarti (1995). *Animal Kingdom*. New Delhi: Discovery Publishing House. ISBN 81-7141-274-2.

Bhaskara Rao, Digumarti (1995). *Batracology*. New Delhi: Discovery Publishing House. ISBN 81-7141-279-3.

Bhaskara Rao, Digumarti (1997). *Scientific Attitude*. New Delhi: Discovery Publishing House. ISBN 81-7141-381-1.

Bhaskara Rao, Digumarti (1996). *Scientific Attitude vis-à-vis Scientific Aptitude*. New Delhi: Discovery Publishing House. ISBN 81-7141-308-0.

Bhaskara Rao, Digumarti (2004). *Scientific Attitude, Scientific Aptitude and Achievement*. New Delhi: Discovery Publishing House. ISBN 81-7141-781-7.

Bhaskara Rao, Digumarti (2004). *Educational Administration*. New Delhi: Discovery Publishing House. ISBN 81-7141-842-2.

Bhaskara Rao, Digumarti, editor (1996). *Encyclopaedia of Education For All*, 5 volumes. New Delhi: APH Publishing Corporation. ISBN 81-7024-759-4 (set).

Vol. I *Education For All: The World Conference*. ISBN 81-7024-760-8.

Vol. II *Education For All: The EPA-9 Summit.* ISBN 81-7024-761-6.

Vol. III *Education For All: Quality Education For All.* ISBN 81-7024-762-6.

Vol. IV *Education For All: Planning and Monitoring.* ISBN 81-7024-763-4.

Vol. V *Education For All: The Indian Scenario.* ISBN 81-7024-764-0.

Bhaskara Rao, Digumarti, editor (1996). *Global Perceptions on Peace Education*, 3 volumes. New Delhi: Discovery Publishing House. ISBN 81-7141-319-6.

Bhaskara Rao, Digumarti, editor (1996). *National Policy on Education*, 2 volumes. New Delhi: Anmol Publications Pvt. Ltd. ISBN 81-7488-323-1.

Bhaskara Rao, Digumarti, editor (1997). *Care the Child*, 2 volumes. New Delhi: Discovery Publishing House. ISBN 81-7141-394-3.

Bhaskara Rao, Digumarti, editor (1997). *Education for the 21st Century*. New Delhi: Discovery Publishing House. ISBN 81-7141-389-7.

Bhaskara Rao, Digumarti, editor (1997). *Reflections on Scientific Attitude*. New Delhi: Discovery Publishing House. ISBN 81-7141-319-6.

Bhaskara Rao, Digumarti, editor (1997). *Success Story of a Primary Education Project*. New Delhi: APH Publishing Corporation. ISBN 81-7024-850-7.

Bhaskara Rao, Digumarti, editor (1997). *World Food Summit.* New Delhi: Discovery Publishing House. ISBN 81-7141-386-2.

Bhaskara Rao, Digumarti, editor (1998). *Adolescence Education.* New Delhi: Discovery Publishing House. ISBN 81-7141-432-X.

Bhaskara Rao, Digumarti, editor (1998). *Community and School Nutrition Education.* New Delhi: Discovery Publishing House. ISBN 81-7141-435-4.

Bhaskara Rao, Digumarti, editor (1998). *District Primary Education Programme*. New Delhi: Discovery Publishing House. ISBN 81-7141-396-X.

Bhaskara Rao, Digumarti, editor (1998). *Earth Summit*, 2 volumes. New Delhi: Discovery Publishing House. ISBN 81-7141-435-4.

Bhaskara Rao, Digumarti, editor (1998). *National Policy on Education: Towards an Enlightened and Humane Society*. New Delhi: Discovery Publishing House. ISBN 81-7141-426-5.

Bhaskara Rao, Digumarti, editor (1998). *Reforming School Education*. New Delhi: Discovery Publishing House. ISBN 81-7141-403-6.

Bhaskara Rao, Digumarti, editor (1998). *Teacher Education in India*. New Delhi: Discovery Publishing House. ISBN 81-7141-406-0.

Bhaskara Rao, Digumarti, editor (1998). *World Summit for Social Development*. New Delhi: Discovery Publishing House. ISBN 81-7141-420-6.

Bhaskara Rao, Digumarti, editor (2000). *Education For All: Achieving the Goal*, 3 volumes. New Delhi: APH Publishing Corporation. ISBN 81-7648-152-1 (set).

Vol. I *The Global Consensus*. ISBN 81-7648-155-6.

Vol. II *Mid-Decade Review Reports of Regional Seminars*. ISBN 81-7648-154-8.

Vol. III *Issues and Trends*. ISBN 81-7648-155-6.

Bhaskara Rao, Digumarti, editor (1999). *International Encyclopaedia of AIDS*, 11 volumes. New Delhi: Discovery Publishing House. ISBN 81-7141-522-6 (set).

Vol. 1 *Introduction to HIV/AIDS*. ISBN 81-7141-523-7.

Vol. 2 *HIV/AIDS-Issues and Challenges*, 2 parts. ISBN 81-7141-524-5.

Vol. 3 *HIV/AIDS-Socio Economic Realities*. ISBN 81-7141-524-3.

Vol. 4 *HIV/AIDS-Law Ethics and Human Rights*, 2 parts. ISBN 81-7141-526-1.

Vol. 5 *AIDS and NGOs*. ISBN 81-7141-527-X.

Vol. 6 *AIDS and Home Care*. ISBN 81-7141-528-8.

Vol. 7 *STD Case Management*. ISBN 81-7141-529-6.

Vol. 8 *HIV/AIDS Prevention and Care-Teaching Modules for Nurses and Midwives*. ISBN 81-7141-530-X.

Vol. 9 *HIV Prevention Education for Educational Institutions*. ISBN 81-7141-531-8.

Vol.10 *Instructional Modules for AIDS Education*. ISBN 81-7141-532-6.

Vol.11 *School Health Education to prevent AIDS and STD-A Package for Curriculum Planners*. ISBN 81-7141-533-4.

Bhaskara Rao, Digumarti, editor (2000). *International Encyclopaedia of Science and Technology Education*, 11 volumes. New Delhi: Discovery Publishing House. ISBN 81-7141-548-2 (set).

Vol. 1 *Science and Technology Education*. ISBN 81-7141-568-7.

Vol. 2 *Science Education in Developing Countries*. ISBN 81-7141-569-9.

Vol. 3 *Organizational Structure of Science*. ISBN 81-7141-570-9.

Vol. 4 *Science Education in Asia and the Pacific*. ISBN 81-7141-571-7

Vol. 5 *Science and Technology Education For All*. ISBN 81-7141-572-5.

Vol. 6 *Values, Ethics, Talent and Girls in Science and Technology Education*. ISBN 81-7141-573-3.

Vol. 7 *Popularization of Science and Technology Education*. ISBN 81-7141-574-1.

Vol. 8 *Science, Power and Society*. ISBN 81-7141-575-X.

Vol. 9 *Information Technology*. ISBN 81-7141-576-8.

Vol. 10 *Teacher Training in Science and Technology Education*. ISBN 81-7142-577-6.

Vol. 11 *Teacher Training in Science and Technology: A Curriculum Framework*. ISBN 81-7141-578-4.

Bhaskara Rao, Digumarti, editor (2001). *Distance Education in Different Countries*. New Delhi: APH Publishing Corporation. ISBN 81-7648-229-3.

Bhaskara Rao, Digumarti, editor (2001). *Decentralised Management of Education: Management of Education in Panchayati Raj and Municipal Bodies*. New Delhi: Discovery Publishing House. ISBN 81-7141-617-9.

Bhaskara Rao, Digumarti, editor (2001). *Electrochemistry for Environmental Protection*. New Delhi: Discovery Publishing House. ISBN 81-7141-619-5.

Bhaskara Rao, Digumarti, editor (2001). *Global Educational Studies*. New Delhi: Discovery Publishing House. ISBN 81-7141-616-0.

Bhaskara Rao, Digumarti, editor (2001). *Global Synthesis of Educational Assessment*. New Delhi: Discovery Publishing House. ISBN 81-7141-613-6.

Bhaskara Rao, Digumarti, editor (2000). *International Encyclopaedia of Human Rights*, 7 volumes in 13 parts. New Delhi: Discovery Publishing House. ISBN 81-7141-567-9 (set).

Vol. 1 *International Instruments of Human Rights*, 2 parts. ISBN 81-7141-569-4.

Vol. 2 *Regional Instruments of Human Rights*. ISBN 81-7141-604-7.

Vol. 3 *Human Rights and the United Nations*, 2 parts. ISBN 81-7141-605-5.

Vol. 4 *Fact Files of Human Rights*, 3 parts. ISBN 81-7141-606-3.

Vol. 5 *Study Stories of Human Rights*, 3 parts. ISBN 81-7141-607-3.

Vol. 6 *International Meetings on Human Rights*, 2 parts.ISBN 81-714-608-X.

Vol. 7 *Professional Training in Human Rights*. ISBN 81-7141-609-8.

Bhaskara Rao, Digumarti, editor (2001). *Jomtein Decade of Education*. New Delhi: Discovery Publishing House. ISBN 81-7141-618-7.

Bhaskara Rao, Digumarti, editor (2001). *Nuclear Materials: Issues and Concerns*, 2 volumes. New Delhi: Discovery Publishing House. ISBN 81-7141-611-X.

Bhaskara Rao, Digumarti, editor (2001). *World Conference on Education for All*. New Delhi: APH Publishing Corporation. ISBN 81-7141-274-9.

Bhaskara Rao, Digumarti, editor (2001). *World Conference on Higher Education*. New Delhi: Discovery Publishing House. ISBN 81-7141-610-1.

Bhaskara Rao, Digumarti, editor (2001). *World Conference on Science*. New Delhi: Discovery Publishing House. ISBN 81-7141-612-8.

Bhaskara Rao, Digumarti, editor (2003). *Inspiring Experiences in Teacher Education*. New Delhi: Discovery Publishing House. ISBN 81-7141-656-X.

Bhaskara Rao, Digumarti, editor (2003). *International Studies in Education*, 3 volumes. New Delhi: Discovery Publishing House. ISBN 81-7141-647-0.

Bhaskara Rao, Digumarti, editor (2003). *Military Conversion: Impact on Science and Technology*. New Delhi: Discovery Publishing House. ISBN 81-7141-578-4.

Bhaskara Rao, Digumarti, editor (2003). *United Nations Millennium Summit*. New Delhi: Discovery Publishing House. ISBN 81-7141-632-2.

Bhaskara Rao, Digumarti, editor (2003). *World Assembly on Aging*. *New Delhi*: Discovery Publishing House. ISBN 81-7141-637-3.

Bhaskara Rao, Digumarti, editor (2003). *World Conference on Human Rights*. New Delhi: Discovery Publishing House. ISBN 81-7141-661-6.

Bhaskara Rao, Digumarti, editor (2003). *World Education Forum*. New Delhi: Discovery Publishing House. ISBN 81-7141-639-X.

Bhaskara Rao, Digumarti, editor (2003). *Education, Employment and Human Resource Development*. New Delhi: Discovery Publishing House. ISBN 81-7141-681-0.

Bhaskara Rao, Digumarti, editor (2003). *Successful Schooling*. New Delhi: Discovery Publishing House. ISBN 81-7141-677-2.

Bhaskara Rao, Digumarti, editor (2003). *European Education and Teachers*. New Delhi: Discovery Publishing House. ISBN 81-7141-702-7.

Bhaskara Rao, Digumarti, editor (2003). *Teachers in a Changing World*. New Delhi: Discovery Publishing House. ISBN 81-7141-694-2.

Bhaskara Rao, Digumarti, editor (2004). *International Encyclopaedia of Learning to Live Together*, 4 volumes. New Delhi: Discovery Publishing House. ISBN 81-7141-848-1.

Vol. 1 *International Conference on Learning to Live Together*.

Vol. 2 *Globalization and Living Together*.

Vol. 3 *Curriculum for Learning to Live Together*.

Vol. 4 *Science Education for the Contemporary Society*.

Bhaskara Rao, Digumarti, editor (2004). *International Guidelines on Open and Distance Teacher Education*. New Delhi: Discovery Publishing House. ISBN 81-7141-777-9.

Bhaskara Rao, Digumarti, editor (2004). *Adult Learning in the 21st Century*. New Delhi: Discovery Publishing House. ISBN 81-7141-797-3.

Bhaskara Rao, Digumarti, editor (2004). *Educational Practices: Research and Recommendations*. New Delhi: Discovery Publishing House. ISBN 81-7141-835-X.

Bhaskara Rao, Digumarti, editor (2004). *General Secondary Education In the 21st Century*. New Delhi: Discovery Publishing House. ISBN 81-7141-885-6.

Bhaskara Rao, Digumarti, editor (2004). *Reforming Secondary Education*. New Delhi: Discovery Publishing House. ISBN 81-7141-843-0.

Bhaskara Rao, Digumarti, editor (2004). *Human Rights Education*. New Delhi: Discovery Publishing House. ISBN 81-7141-882-1.

Bhaskara Rao, Digumarti, editor (2004). *United Nations Decade for Human Rights Education*. New Delhi: Discovery Publishing House. ISBN 81-7141-887-2.

Bhaskara Rao, Digumarti and B.S.V. Dutt, editors (2003). *Education: Programmes and Policies*. New Delhi: APH Publishing Corporation. ISBN 81-7648-470-9.

Bhaskara Rao, Digumarti, C.A.P. Swamy and B.S.V. Dutt (1997). *Self-Evaluation in Student Teaching*. New Delhi: Discovery Publishing House. ISBN 81-7141-374-9.

Bhaskara Rao, Digumarti and D. Naresh Kumar (2004). *School Teacher Effectiveness*. New Delhi: Discovery Publishing House. ISBN 81-7141-782-5.

Bhaskara Rao, Digumarti and D. Sridhar (2002). *Job Satisfaction of School Teachers*. New Delhi: Discovery Publishing House. ISBN 81-7141-652-7.

Bhaskara Rao, Digumarti, C. Sridevi and K. Vijaya (1995). *Achievement in Social Studies*. New Delhi: Discovery Publishing House. ISBN 81-7141-281-5.

Bhaskara Rao, Digumarti and Digumarti Pushpa Latha (1994). *Achievement in Biology*. New Delhi: Discovery Publishing House. ISBN 81-7141-264-5.

Bhaskara Rao, Digumarti and Digumarti Pushpa Latha (1995). *Achievement in English*. New Delhi: Discovery Publishing House. ISBN 81-7141-283-1.

Bhaskara Rao, Digumarti and Digumarti Pushpa Latha (1994). *Achievement in Science*. New Delhi: Discovery Publishing House. ISBN 81-7141-280-70.

Bhaskara Rao, Digumarti and Digumarti Pushpa Latha (1995). *Achievement in Mathematics*. New Delhi: Discovery Publishing House. ISBN 81-7141-278-5.

Bhaskara Rao, Digumarti and Digumarti Pushpa Latha (2004). *Education for Women*. New Delhi: Discovery Publishing House. ISBN 81-7141-873-2.

Bhaskara Rao, Digumarti and Digumarti Pushpa Latha, editors (1998). *International Encyclopaedia of Women*, 5 volumes. New Delhi: Discovery Publishing House. ISBN 81-7141-410-9 (set).

Vol. 1 *Status of World's Women*. ISBN 81-7141-494-X.

Vol. 2 *Women, Education and Empowerment*. ISBN 81-7141-498-1.

Vol. 3 *Women Challenges and Advancement*. ISBN 81-7141-497-4.

Vol. 4 *Women and Family Health*. ISBN 81-7141-497-4.

Vol. 5 *Women and International Action*. ISBN 81-7141-498-2.

Bhaskara Rao, Digumarti, Digumarti Pushpa Latha and Digumarthi Harshitha, editors (2001). *Biological Warfare*. New Delhi: Discovery Publishing House. ISBN 81-7141-597-0.

Bhaskara Rao, Digumarti, Digumarti Pushpa Latha and Digumarthi Harshitha, editors (2001). *Women as Educators*. New Delhi: Discovery Publishing House. ISBN 81-7141-602-0.

Bhaskara Rao, Digumarti and Digumarthi Harshitha (2004). *Adjustment of Adolescents*. New Delhi: APH Publishing House. ISBN 81-7648-836-8.

Bhaskara Rao, Digumarti and Digumarthi Harshitha, editors (2001). *Education in India*. New Delhi: APH Publishing House. ISBN 81-7648-207-2.

Bhaskara Rao, Digumarti, Digumarti Pushpa Latha and Digumarthi Harshitha, editors (2001). *Assessing Learning Achievement*. New Delhi: Discovery Publishing House. ISBN 81-7141-601-2.

Bhaskara Rao, Digumarti, Digumarti Pushpa Latha and Digumarthi Harshitha, editors (2001). *Energy Security*. New Delhi: Discovery Publishing House. ISBN 81-7141-598-9.

Bhaskara Rao, Digumarti, Digumarthi Harshitha and K.R.S. Sambasiva Rao, editors (1999). *Advanced Biotechnology*. New Delhi: Discovery Publishing House. ISBN 81-7141-516-4.

Bhaskara Rao, Digumarti and K.R.S.Sambasiva Rao, editors (1996). *Current Trends in Indian Education*. New Delhi: Discovery Publishing House. ISBN 81-7141-311-0.

Bhaskara Rao, Digumarti and D. Naresh Kumar (2004). *School Teacher Effectiveness*. New Delhi: Discovery Publishing House. ISBN 81-7141-782-5.

Bhaskara Rao, Digumarti and E. Sreekanth Babu (2004). *Educational Interests of School Students*. New Delhi: Discovery Publishing House. ISBN 81-7141-837-6.

Bhaskara Rao, Digumarti and K. Vijaya (1995). *A Text Book Evaluation*. Ambala Cantt: The Associated Publishers.

Bhaskara Rao, Digumarti and M.A. Fayaz (2004). *Problems of Primary School Drop-outs*. New Delhi: Discovery Publishing House. ISBN 81-7141-834-1.

Bhaskara Rao, Digumarti and N.V.M. Mohana Rao (2002). *Problems of Mentally Handicapped Children*. New Delhi: Discovery Publishing House. ISBN 81-7141-645-4.

Bhaskara Rao, Digumarti and S. Chandra Mohan (2002). *Sports Management*. New Delhi: APH Publishing House. ISBN 81-7648-467-9.

Bhaskara Rao, Digumarti and S.A. Khader (2004). *Problems of Private School Teachers*. New Delhi: Discovery Publishing House. ISBN 81-7141-838-4.

Bhaskara Rao, Digumarti and S.A. Khader (2004). *School Education in India*. New Delhi: Discovery Publishing House. ISBN 81-7141-849-X.

Bhaskara Rao, Digumarti and Sk. Johni Basha (2004). *Teachers' Population Education Awareness*. New Delhi: Discovery Publishing House. ISBN 81-7141-832-5.

Bhaskara Rao, Digumarti, V.V. Rao, V.V. Lakshmi and V.V. Krishna, editors (1999). *Status and Advancement of Women*. New Delhi: APH Publishing Corporation. ISBN 81-7648-169-6.

Babu, P.C., author and Digumarti Bhaskara Rao, editor (2004). *Flowers of Wisdom*. New Delhi: Discovery Publishing House. ISBN 81-7141-695-0.

Amala, P.A. and Anupam, P., authors and Digumarti Bhaskara Rao, editor (2004). *History of Education*. New Delhi: Discovery Publishing House. ISBN 81-7141-860-0.

Bhagya Lakshmi, L., author and Digumarti Bhaskara Rao, editor (2000). *Reading and Comprehension*. New Delhi: Discovery Publishing House. ISBN 81-7141-543-1.

Bhasha, S.A., author and Digumarti Bhaskara Rao, editor (2004). *Methods of Teaching Geography*. New Delhi: Discovery Publishing House. ISBN 81-7141-807-4.

Bhuvaneswara Lakshmi, Gadde, author and Digumarti Bhaskara Rao, editor (2000). *Attitude Towards Science*. New Delhi: Discovery Publishing House. ISBN 81-7141-541-6.

Bhuvaneswari Lakshmi, G., author and Digumarti Bhaskara Rao, editor (2004). *Methods of Teaching Life Science*. New Delhi: Discovery Publishing House. ISBN 81-7141-804-X.

Bhuvaneswari Lakshmi, G. and K. Subba Rao, authors and Digumarti Bhaskara Rao, editor (2004). *Methods of Teaching Biology*. New Delhi: Discovery Publishing House. ISBN 81-7141-914-3.

Chowdary, S.B.J.R. and Naga Raju authors and Digumarti Bhaskara Rao, editor (2004). *Mastery of Teaching Skills*. New Delhi: Discovery Publishing House. ISBN 81-7141-861-9.

Devraj, T.A.S., author and Digumarti Bhaskara Rao, editor (1997). *Trace Analysis of Uranium and Thorium*. New Delhi: Discovery Publishing House. ISBN 81-7141-375-7.

Durga Rani, K., author and Digumarti Bhaskara Rao, editor (2000). *Educational Aspirations and Scientific Attitudes*. New Delhi: Discovery Publishing House. ISBN 81-7141-555-5.

Dutt, B.S.V. and Digumarti Bhaskara Rao (2001). *Empowering Primary Teachers*. New Delhi: Discovery Publishing House. ISBN 81-7141-615-2.

Dutt, B.S.V., author and Digumarti Bhaskara Rao, editor (2004). *Comparative Education*. New Delhi: Discovery Publishing House. ISBN 81-7141-912-7.

Ediger, Marlow and Digumarti Bhaskara Rao (1996). *Science Curriculum*. New Delhi: Discovery Publishing House. ISBN 81-7141-321-8.

Ediger, Marlow and Digumarti Bhaskara Rao (2000). *Teaching Mathematics Successfully*. New Delhi: Discovery Publishing House. ISBN 81-7141-552-0.

Ediger, Marlow and Digumarti Bhaskara Rao (2001). *Teaching Science Successfully*. New Delhi: Discovery Publishing House. ISBN 81-7141-600-4.

Ediger, Marlow and Digumarti Bhaskara Rao (2001). *Teaching Social Studies Successfully*. New Delhi: Discovery Publishing House. ISBN 81-7141-596-2.

Ediger, Marlow and Digumarti Bhaskara Rao (2002). *Philosophy and Curriculum*. New Delhi: Discovery Publishing House. ISBN 81-7141-631-4.

Ediger, Marlow and Digumarti Bhaskara Rao (2002). *Improving School Administration*. New Delhi: Discovery Publishing House. ISBN 81-7141-633-0.

Ediger, Marlow and Digumarti Bhaskara Rao (2002). *Elementary Curriculum*. New Delhi: Discovery Publishing House. ISBN 81-7141-658-6.

Ediger, Marlow and Digumarti Bhaskara Rao (2003). *Language Arts Curriculum*. New Delhi: Discovery Publishing House. ISBN 81-7141-657-8.

Ediger, Marlow and Digumarti Bhaskara Rao (2003). *Psychology and Curriculum*. New Delhi: Discovery Publishing House. ISBN 81-7141-691-8.

Ediger, Marlow and Digumarti Bhaskara Rao (2003). *Teaching Language Arts Successfully*. New Delhi: Discovery Publishing House. ISBN 81-7141-678-0.

Ediger, Marlow and Digumarti Bhaskara Rao (2003). *School Curriculum and Administration*. New Delhi: Discovery Publishing House. ISBN 81-7141-709-4.

Ediger, Marlow and Digumarti Bhaskara Rao (2003). *Teaching Mathematics in Elementary Schools*. New Delhi: Discovery Publishing House. ISBN 81-7141-687-X.

Ediger, Marlow and Digumarti Bhaskara Rao (2003). Teaching Science in Elementary Schools. New Delhi: Discovery Publishing House. ISBN 81-7141-698-5.

Ediger, Marlow and Digumarti Bhaskara Rao (2003). *School Curriculum and Administration*. New Delhi: Discovery Publishing House. ISBN 81-7141-709-4.

Ediger, Marlow and Digumarti Bhaskara Rao (2003). *Elementary Curriculum Improvement*. New Delhi: Discovery Publishing House. ISBN 81-7141-740-X.

Ediger, Marlow and Digumarti Bhaskara Rao (2004). *School Organisation*. New Delhi: Discovery Publishing House. ISBN 81-7141-843-0.

Ediger, Marlow and Digumarti Bhaskara Rao (2004). *Relevancy in Elementary Curriculum*. New Delhi: Discovery Publishing House. ISBN 81-7141-845-9.

Ediger, Marlow, B.S.V. Dutt and Digumarti Bhaskara Rao (2003). *Teaching English Successfully*. New Delhi: Discovery Publishing House. ISBN 81-7141-707-8.

Elizabeth, M.E.S., author and Digumarti Bhaskara Rao, editor (2004). *Methods of Teaching English*. New Delhi: Discovery Publishing House. ISBN 81-7141-809-0.

Harshitha, D. author and Digumarti Bhaskara Rao, editor (2004). *Methods of Teaching Information Technology*. New Delhi: Discovery Publishing House. ISBN 81-7141-805-8.

Indira Devi, author and J. Prasanth Kumar and Digumarti Bhaskara Rao, editors (2004). *Values in Language Text Books*. New Delhi: APH Publishing Corporation. ISBN 81-7141-833-3.

Jalaja Kumari, C., author and Digumarti Bhaskara Rao, editor (2004). *Methods of Teaching Educational Technology*. New Delhi: Discovery Publishing House. ISBN 81-7141-810-4.

Jayasree, Kandi, author and Digumarti Bhaskara Rao, editor (1999). *Correlates of Socialisation*. New Delhi: Discovery Publishing House. ISBN 81-7141-517-2.

Jayasree, Kandi, author and Digumarti Bhaskara Rao, editor (2004). *Methods of Teaching Science*. New Delhi: Discovery Publishing House. ISBN 81-7141-801-5.

John Babu, Chikati, author and T.J.R. Prasad, G.M. Madhukar and Digumarti Bhaskara Rao, editors (1996). *Problem Solving in Mathematics*. New Delhi: APH Publishing Corporation. ISBN 81-7648-273-0.

Joseph Raju, B and G.A. Anitha, authors and Digumarti Bhaskara Rao, editor (2004). *Population Education*. New Delhi: Sonali Publications. ISBN 81-88836-31-3.

Lalitha, T., author and K.S. Prabhakaram, D.S.N. Sastry and Digumarti Bhaskara Rao, editors (2004). *Educational Philosophic Beliefs*. New Delhi: Discovery Publishing House. ISBN 81-7141-765-5.

Madhu Bala, Jampala, author and Digumarti Bhaskara Rao, editor (2004). *Adjustment Problems of Hearing Impaired*. New Delhi: Discovery Publishing House. ISBN 81-7141-831-7.

Madhu Bala, Jampala, author and Digumarti Bhaskara Rao, editor (2004). *Methods of Teaching Exceptional Children*. New Delhi: Discovery Publishing House. ISBN 81-7141-802-3.

Marja, Talvi and Digumarti Bhaskara Rao, editors (1996). *Educational Leadership and Social Changes*. New Delhi: Discovery Publishing House. ISBN 81-7141-320-X.

Nageswara Rao, S.and M. Srihari, authors and Digumarti Bhaskara Rao, editor (2004). *Guidance and Counselling*. New Delhi: Discovery Publishing House. ISBN 81-7141-840-6.

Nageswara Rao, S. and P. Sridhar, authors and Digumarti Bhaskara Rao, editor (2004). *Methods and Techniques of Teaching*. New Delhi: Sonali Publications. ISBN 81-88836-33-8.

Nirmala Jyothi, M., author and Digumarti Bhaskara Rao, editor (2003). *Non-detention System in School Education*. New Delhi: Discovery Publishing House. ISBN 81-7141-654-3.

Padma Tulasi, G., author and Digumarti Bhaskara Rao, editor (2004). *Methods of Teaching Elementary Science*. New Delhi: Discovery Publishing House. ISBN 81-7141-871-6.

Pala Prasada Rao, V., author and K. Nirupa Rani and Digumarti Bhaskara Rao, editors (2004). *Methods of Teaching Elementary Science*. New Delhi: Discovery Publishing House. ISBN 81-7141-871-6.

Prabhakaram, K.S., author and Digumarti Bhaskara Rao, editors (1998). *Concept Attainment Model in Mathematics Teaching*. New Delhi: Discovery Publishing House. ISBN 81-7141-424-9.

Prasanth Kumar, J., author and Digumarti Bhaskara Rao, editor (1998). *Effectiveness of Distance Education System*. New Delhi: Discovery Publishing House. ISBN 81-7141-437-0.

Prasanth Kumar, J., author and Digumarti Bhaskara Rao, editor (2004). *Methods of Teaching Civics*. New Delhi: Discovery Publishing House. ISBN 81-7141-806-6.

Prasanth Kumar, J., author and G. Sundara Rao and Digumarti Bhaskara Rao, editors (2000). *Open University Student Support Services*. New Delhi: Discovery Publishing House. ISBN 81-7141-550-4.

Raja Kumari, M.A. and D.R.S. Sundari, authors and Digumarti Bhaskara Rao, editor (2004). *Special Education*. New Delhi: Discovery Publishing House. ISBN 81-7141-846-5.

Raja Kumari, M.A. and D.R.S. Sundari, authors and Digumarti Bhaskara Rao, editor (2004). *Methods of Teaching Educational Psychology*. New Delhi: Discovery Publishing House. ISBN 81-7141-820-1.

Ramatulasamma, K., author and Digumarti Bhaskara Rao, editor (2002). *Job Satisfaction of Teacher Educators*. New Delhi: Discovery Publishing House. ISBN 81-7141-655-1.

Rama Krishnaiah, D., author and Digumarti Bhaskara Rao, editor (1998). *Job Satisfaction of College Teachers*. New Delhi: Discovery Publishing House. ISBN 81-7141-438-9.

Rama Kumar Ratnam, M.V., author and Digumarti Bhaskara Rao, editor (1998). *Dukkha: Suffering in Early Buddhism*. New Delhi: Discovery Publishing House. ISBN 81-7141-653-5.

Rama Krishna Prasad and P. Vide Sagar, authors and Digumarti Bhaskara Rao, editor (2004). *Methods of Teaching Physical Education*. New Delhi: Discovery Publishing House. ISBN 81-7141-868-6.

Rama Seshaiah, P. author and Digumarti Bhaskara Rao, editor (2004). *Methods of Teaching Home Science*. New Delhi: Discovery Publishing House. ISBN 81-7141-916-X.

Ramesh, Ganta and Digumarti Bhaskara Rao, editors (1998). *Environmental Education: Problems and Prospects*. New Delhi: Discovery Publishing House. ISBN 81-7141-423-0.

Ranga Rao, R., author and Digumarti Bhaskara Rao, editor (2004). *Methods of Teacher Teaching*. New Delhi: Discovery Publishing House. ISBN 81-7141-812-0.

Rathaiah, Lavu and Digumarti Bhaskara Rao, editors (1996), *International Innovations in Education*. New Delhi: Discovery Publishing House. ISBN 81-7141-359-5.

Rathaiah, Lavu and Digumarti Bhaskara Rao (1997). *Achievement Correlates*. New Delhi: Discovery Publishing House. ISBN 81-7141-385-4.

Ravi Krishna, M., author and Digumarti Bhaskara Rao, editor (2004). *Examination System*. New Delhi: Discovery Publishing House. ISBN 81-7141-824-4.

Ravi Kumar, M., author and Digumarti Bhaskara Rao, editor (2004). *Methods of Teaching Computer Science*. New Delhi: Discovery Publishing House. ISBN 81-7141-823-6.

Reddy, Sudhakar Y., author and Digumarti Bhaskara Rao, editor (2003). *Creativity in Adolescents*. New Delhi: Discovery Publishing House. ISBN 81-7141-659-4.

Reddy, M. S., author and Digumarti Bhaskara Rao, editor (2004). *Creativity in College Students*. New Delhi: Discovery Publishing House. ISBN 81-7141-697-7.

Rudramamba, B., author and Digumarti Bhaskara Rao, editor (2003). *Problems of Teaching*. New Delhi: APH Publishing Corporation. ISBN 81-7648-462-8.

Rudramamba, B. and V. Lakshmi Kumari, authors and Digumarti Bhaskara Rao, editor (2004). *Methods of Teaching Economics*. New Delhi: Discovery Publishing House. ISBN 81-7141-900-3.

Sanjeeva Rao, P.C., author and Digumarti Bhaskara Rao, editor (1996). *A Text Book of Geology*. New Delhi: Discovery Publishing House. ISBN 81-7141-313-7.

Satya Narayana, V., author and Digumarti Bhaskara Rao, editor (2001). *Physical Education, Social Attitudes and Leadership Qualities*. New Delhi: Discovery Publishing House. ISBN 81-7141-593-8.

Satya Narayana, P.V.V. and G. Krishna, authors and Digumarti Bhaskara Rao, editor (2004). *Curriculum Development and Management*. New Delhi: Discovery Publishing House. ISBN 81-7141-813-9.

Siva Lakshmi, G.V. and G.L. Subbaiah, authors and Digumarti Bhaskara Rao, editor (2004). *Methods of Teaching Environmental Science*. New Delhi: Discovery Publishing House. ISBN 81-7141-839-2.

Srinivas, M. and I. Prasada Rao, authors and Digumarti Bhaskara Rao, editor (2004). *Methods of Teaching History*. New Delhi: Discovery Publishing House. ISBN 81-7141-803-1.

Srinivasulu Reddy, M. and K.R.S. Sambasiva Rao, authors and Digumarti Bhaskara Rao, editor (1999). *A Text Book of Aquaculture*. New Delhi: Discovery Publishing House. ISBN 81-7141-482-6.

Srinivasa Rao, Mandalapu, author and Digumarti Bhaskara Rao, editor (2003). *Achievement Motivation and Achievement in Mathematics*. New Delhi: Discovery Publishing House. ISBN 81-7141-674-8.

Sunil Kumar, K. and K. Rama Krishana, authors and Digumarti Bhaskara Rao, editor (2004). *Methods of Teaching Chemistry*. New Delhi: Discovery Publishing House. ISBN 81-7141-913-5.

Sunita, E. and R. Sambasiva Rao, authors and Digumarti Bhaskara Rao, editor (2004). *Methods of Teaching Mathematics*. New Delhi: Discovery Publishing House. ISBN 81-7141-915-1.

Swarupa Rani, T. and J.R. Priyadarshini, authors and Digumarti Bhaskara Rao, editor (2004). *Educational Measurement and Evaluation*. New Delhi: Discovery Publishing House. ISBN 81-7141-859-7.

Vanaja, M., author and Digumarti Bhaskara Rao, editor (1999). *Inquiry Training Model*. New Delhi: Discovery Publishing House. ISBN 81-7141-515-6.

Vanaja, M., author and Digumarti Bhaskara Rao, editor (2004). *Methods of Teaching Physics*. New Delhi: Discovery Publishing House. ISBN 81-7141-867-8.

Valeri V. Koustiouk, author and Digumarti Bhaskara Rao, editor (2002). *A Text Book of Cryogenics*. New Delhi: Discovery Publishing House. ISBN 81-7141-642-X.

Vamsi Krishana, V., author and Digumarti Bhaskara Rao, editor (2004). *School Psychology*. New Delhi: Discovery Publishing House. ISBN 81-7141-880-5.

Veena Kumari, Balusu and Digumarti Bhaskara Rao (1996). *Operation Black Board*. New Delhi: APH Publishing Corporation. ISBN 81-7024-711-X.

Veena Kumari, B. author and Digumarti Bhaskara Rao, editor (2004). *Methods of Teaching Social Studies*. New Delhi: Discovery Publishing House. ISBN 81-7141-899-6.

Veena Kumari, Balusu, author and Digumarti Bhaskara Rao, editor (2000). *Psycho-Social Correlates of Achievement*. New Delhi: Discovery Publishing House. ISBN 81-7141-547-4.

Venkata Rao, P. and Digumarti Bhaskara Rao (1989). *A Text Book of Zoology-Junior Intermediate*. Guntur: Vignan Publishers.

Venkata Rao, P. and Digumarti Bhaskara Rao (1989). *A Text Book of Zoology-Senior Intermediate*. Guntur: Vignan Publishers.

Venkateswara Reddy, L. and Lakshmi Narayana, M., authors and Digumarti Bhaskara Rao, editor (2004). *Methods of Teaching Rural Sociology*. New Delhi: Discovery Publishing House. ISBN 81-7141-811-2.

Venkateswara Rao, V., author and Digumarti Bhaskara Rao, editor (2004). *Problems of Education*. New Delhi: Discovery Publishing House. ISBN 81-7141-841-4.

Venkateswara Rao, V., V. Vijaya Lakshmi and V. Vamsi Krishna, authors and Digumarti Bhaskara Rao, editor (2004). *Education For All*. New Delhi: Sonali Publications. ISBN 81-88836-30-3.

Venkateswara Rao, V., V. Vijaya Lakshmi and V. Vamsi Krishna, authors and Digumarti Bhaskara Rao, editor (2004). *Education in India*. New Delhi: Sonali Publications. ISBN 81-88836-858-9.

Venkateswara Reddy, L. and Lakshmi Narayana, M., authors and Digumarti Bhaskara Rao, editor (2004). *Education for Dalits*. New Delhi: Discovery Publishing House. ISBN 81-7141-872-4.

Venkateswarlu, K. and S.J. Basha, authors and Digumarti Bhaskara Rao, editor (2004). *Methods of Teaching Commerce*. New Delhi: Discovery Publishing House. ISBN 81-7141-808-2.

Venugopala Rao, K., author and Digumarti Bhaskara Rao, editor (2000). *Teacher Morale in Secondary Schools*. New Delhi: Discovery Publishing House. ISBN 81-7141-551-2.

Vidya, C., author and Digumarti Bhaskara Rao, editor (1996). *A Text Book of Nutrition*. New Delhi: Discovery Publishing House. ISBN 81-7141-309-9.

Vijaya Bharathi, D., author and Digumarti Bhaskara Rao, editor (2000). *Educational Philosophies of Swami Vivekananda and John Dewey*. New Delhi: APH Publishing House. ISBN 81-7648-309-9.

Vijaya Lakshmi, D., author and Digumarti Bhaskara Rao, editor (2004) *Basic Education*. New Delhi: Discovery Publishing House. ISBN 81-7141-881-3.

Books in Telugu Language

Bhaskara Rao, Digumarti (1986). *Dhrushya Sravana Bodhanapakaranalu (Audio Visual Teaching Aids)*. Guntur: Nagarjuna Publishers.

Bhaskara Rao, Digumarti (1993). *Jeevasashtra Bodhana (Teaching of Biology)*. Guntur: Nagarjuna Publishers.

Bhaskara Rao, Digumarti (1995). *Vignanasasthra Bodhana (Teaching of science)* Guntur: Nagarjuna Publishers.

Bhaskara Rao, Digumarti (1997). *Vidya Manovignana Seshtram (Educational Psychology)*. Guntur: Creative Press.

Bhaskara Rao, Digumarti (1998). *DSC Study Material*. Guntur: Nagarjuna Publishers.

Bhaskara Rao, Digumarti (1998). *Upadhyayudu Vidya. (Teacher and Education)* Guntur: Nagarjuna Publishers.

Bhaskara Rao, Digumarti (1998). *Vidya Drukpadalu (Perspectives of Education)*. Guntur: Nagarjuna Publishers.

Bhaskara Rao, Digumarti (1999). *EdCET Teaching Aptitude*. Guntur: Nagarjuna Publishers.

Bhaskara Rao, Digumarti (2001). *Bharata Samajamulo Upadyayudu Vidya (Teacher and Education in Emerging Indian Society)*. Guntur: Sri Nagarjuna Publishers.

Bhaskara Rao, Digumarti (2001). *Bhoutika Sastra Bodhana Paddathulu (Methods of Teaching Physical Science)*. Guntur: Sri Nagarjuna Publishers.

Bhaskara Rao, Digumarti (2001). *Jeeva Sastra Bodhana Padhathulu (Methods of Teaching Biology)*. Guntur: Sri Nagarjuna Publishers.

Bhaskara Rao, Digumarti (2001). *Vidya Manovignana Sastram (Educational Psychology)*. Guntur: Sri Nagarjuna Publishers.

Bhaskara Rao, Digumarti (2003). *Patasala Yajamanyam / Paripalana (School Management and Administration)*. Guntur: Sri Nagarjuna Publishers.

Gopala Krishna, G., A. Ramkrishna, K. Subba Rao and Bhaskara Rao, Digumarti (2004). *Jeevasashtra Bodhana Padhatulu (Methods of Teaching of Biological science)*. Guntur: Sri Nagarjuna Publishers.

Krishna Murthy, V., K.S. Sudheer Reddy and Digumarti Bhaskara Rao (2004). *Vidya Manovignana Sastra Adharalu (Foundations of Educational Psychology)*. Guntur: Sri Nagarjuna Publishers.

Lalini, V., V. Dayakara Reddy, M. Srihari and Digumarti Bhaskara Rao (2004). *Vidya Adharalu (Foundations of Education)*. Guntur: Sri Nagarjuna Publishers.

Subba Rao, K.P., P. Ayodhya and Digumarti Bhaskara Rao (2004). *Patasala Yajamanyam-Vidhya Vyavasthalu (School Management and Systems of Education)*. Guntur: Sri Nagarjuna Publishers.

Sudhakar, V., B. Ravindra Babu, D.S. Kumar and Digumarti Bhaskara Rao (2004). *Vidya Sanketika Sastram-Computer Vidya (Educational Technology and Computer Education)*. Guntur: Sri Nagarjuna Publishers.

Index